50 HEALTHY, DELICIOUS, LOW-SODIUM, SCHOOL-READY, EASY-TO-MAKE BREAKFAST, SNACK, & LUNCHTIME RECIPES

DASH KIDS LUNCH BREAK

EVA ILIANA

Let Us Know Your Thoughts

Thank you for downloading our ebook. We hope you love it!

If you find our cookbook to be helpful, write a review! We love hearing your feedback so we can provide excellent services and help potential users to make positive decisions.

Thank you in advance for your feedback and for being a valued reader. Reviews help us improve our services and let others know that we care about providing accurate and helpful information.

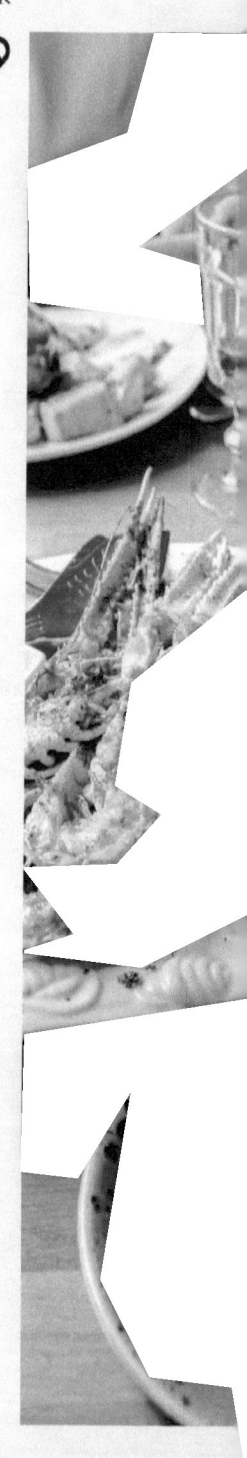

Contents

Introduction —————————————————————— 11

Introduction —————————————————————— 13

Chapter 1: Food as our Foundation ————— 16

The Foundation of Food ———————————————— 21

Macronutrients ——————————————————————— 21

Types of Macronutrients ——————————————— 22

Macronutrients ——————————————————————— 29

Minerals ——————————————————————————— 32

Chapter 2: Your Role as a Parent ————— 33

Foods to Avoid ——————————————————————— 34

Tips and Tricks for Maintaining a HealthyDiet ——— 37

Grocery Shopping for Healthy Kids ————————— 39

Tips for Leading Healthy Eating Habits as a ———— 43

 Parent ——————————————————————————— 43

The Don'ts of Being a Model Parent ———————— 48

The Dos of Model Parenting ————————————— 49

Chapter 3: Letting Them Be The Chef ——— 52

How to Engage Your Children in Cooking ————— 54

Tips for Dealing With Kids Under Age Five ———— 54

Dealing With Kids Above Eight ——————————— 55

Making The Most of Family Time —————————— 56

Building a Family Culture Around Cooking ———— 61

Kitchen Safety -- 63
Safety for Baby Chefs -------------------------------- 64
General Safety and Hygiene ------------------------- 64
Tips for Cooking With Kids -------------------------- 67
Chapter 4: Breakfast Recipes ------------------ 72
Parisian Ham and Cheese Egg Cups ---------------- 74
Quiche Lorraine With Hash Brown Crust ---------- 75
Sunny-Side Up Pizza --------------------------------- 77
Granola Bars -- 78
Salmon and Dill Egg Cups --------------------------- 79
Quiche Biscuits With Bacon, Cheddar, and ------- 80
Chives -- 80
Yogurt Parfaits --------------------------------------- 81
Ham and Cheese Scones ---------------------------- 82
Egg Pepper Rings With Carrot Salsa --------------- 83
Salsa and Sausage Egg Cups ----------------------- 84
Baked and Spiced Oatmeal -------------------------- 85
Banana Cream Pie Overnight Oats ------------------ 86
Apple-Raisin French Toast -------------------------- 87
Gluten-Free Stewed Peppers and Toma-toes ---- 88
With Eggs --- 88
Ham Casserole --------------------------------------- 89
Tater Tot Pizza --------------------------------------- 90
Peanut Butter and Jelly Bars ----------------------- 91

Pimiento, Cheese, and Ham ---------- 92

Scramble ---------- 92

Cheese and Herb Quiche ---------- 93

Lemon Poppy Seed Jelly Doughnuts ---------- 95

Raspberry Smoothie Bowls ---------- 97

Buttermilk Waffle, Bacon, and Egg Sandwich ---------- 98

Sugared Waffles With Sautéed ---------- 99

Maple Apples ---------- 99

Eggs and Tater Bake ---------- 100

French Toast Bowls ---------- 101

Boursin, Bacon, and Spinach Scrambled Eggs ---------- 102

Mexican Scrambled Eggs ---------- 103

Apple Spice Baked Oatmeal ---------- 104

Carrot Cake Oatmeal ---------- 105

Chapter 5: Lunch Recipes ---------- *106*

Hummus Avocado Wrap ---------- 108

Cheddar Apple and Quesadillas ---------- 109

Beef Burritos ---------- 110

Asian Rice Salad ---------- 111

Chicken Noodle Soup ---------- 112

Strawberry Spinach Salad With Red ---------- 113

WineVinaigrette ---------- 113

Pasta With Caruso Sauce ---------- 114

Vegetable Beef Soup ---------- 115

Honeyed Fruit Salad ---------- 116

Chicken Waldorf Sandwiches ---------------------------- 117
Easy Banana Muffins ---------------------------------- 118
Potato and Ham Soup With Cheese---------------------- 119
Vegetable Fried Rice With Spinach---------------------- 120
Horiatiki Salata -------------------------------------- 121
Cucumber Cream Cheese Tea Sandwiches-------------- 122
Macaroni and Cheese Casserole ---------------------- 123
With Ground Beef ------------------------------------ 123
Slow Cooker Taco Soup ------------------------------ 124
Tomato Soup--- 125
Caprese Salad-- 126
Chicken Salad With Grapes -------------------------- 127
Cold Soba Noodle Salad ------------------------------ 128
Mac and Cheese Muffins------------------------------ 129
Crispy Chicken Tenders ------------------------------ 130
Greek Mini Frittatas---------------------------------- 131
Spinach Cashew Pesto-------------------------------- 132
Crock Pot Hamburger Soup -------------------------- 133
Tofu and Egg Salad ---------------------------------- 134

Chapter6: Snacking Like a Boss--------------- 135

Sweet Spinach Muffins ------------------------------ 136
No-Bake Date Bar------------------------------------ 137
Homemade Teething --------------------------------- 138
Zucchini Oat Muffins -------------------------------- 139
Banana Bread --------------------------------------- 140

Strawberry Watermelon Smoothie --------------------------- 141
Whipped Pineapple Pops ----------------------------------- 142
Slow Cooker Applesauce ----------------------------------- 143
Quinoa Pizza Bites -- 144
Banana Roll-Ups -- 145
Parmesan Sweet Potato ----------------------------------- 146
Zucchini Tots --- 146
Strawberry Kiwi Gummies --------------------------------- 147
Kettle Corn --- 148
Red Ants on a Log -- 149
Potato Cakes --- 150
Fresh Fruit and Yogurt Ice Pops -------------------------- 151
Chunky Monkey Pancakes -------------------------------- 152
Conclusion -- 153
References -- 154

© Copyright 2020 - All rights reserved.

The content contained within this book may not be reproduced, duplicated or transmitted without direct written permission from the author or the publisher.Under no circumstances will any blame or legal responsibility be held against the publisher, or author, for any damages, reparation, or monetary loss due to the information contained within this book, either directly or indirectly.

Legal Notice:

This book is copyright protected. It is only for personal use. You cannot amend, distribute, sell, use, quote or paraphrase any part, or the content within this book, without the consent of the author or publisher.

Disclaimer Notice:

Please note the information contained within this document is for educational and entertainment purposes only. All effort has been executed to present accurate, up to date, reliable, complete information. No warranties of any kind are declared or implied. Readers acknowledge that the author is not engaged in the rendering of legal, financial, medical or professional advice. The content within this book has been derived from various sources. Please consult a licensed professional before attempting any techniques outlined in this book.

By reading this document, the reader agrees that under no circumstances is the author responsible for any losses, direct or indirect, that are incurred as a result of the use of the information contained within this document, including, but not limited to, errors, omissions, or inaccuracies.

Introduction

If you've been trying to shed a few pounds, it may interest you to know that 75% of this process relies on the nature of your diet: exercise only accounts for 25% (Huffpost, 2014). This implies that if one is not careful and particular about what goes into their mouths—even the most strenuous physical activities to maintain or reduce weight—might not achieve much.

Now, of all the diets you will hear or read about, the DASH diet has proven to be healthier and more effective than the fads that are often advertised. In fact, it was named the best overall diet in 2018 by the U.S. News & World Report and the second-best in 2020. It should come as no surprise that the DASH diet has achieved this level of success since it was developed by accomplished medical professionals, nutritionists, and statisticians in the United States. This also means that while most diets are often best suited for certain age groups or sexes, the DASH diet works for everyone effectively.

Dietary Approaches to Stop Hypertension or DASH is not about meal restrictions, nor was it created with weight loss as the objective. Instead, as the name suggests, it was developed in response to the alarming increase in high blood pressure cases. Even teenagers and little kids are frequently diagnosed with high blood pressure. According to the World Health Organization, hypertension is one of the leading causes of early deaths all around the world, and as of 2019, roughly 1.13 billion people in various countries are hypertensive (World Health Organization, 2019). These numbers are, indeed, disturbing, leading us to appreciate the efforts that went into researching a preventative and curative dietary method for high blood pressure.

However, this diet plan does not only help manage hypertension. As a result of portion control and its characteristic low sodium and low trans fat meals, DASH is also especially effective at helping people healthily lose weight.

One of the biggest reasons people eventually give up on dieting is because they find it difficult to keep up with the extreme meal restrictions and seemingly unsustainable portion sizes of most diet plans. This can be trickier if you are a 9-to-5er or someone who is just too busy to properly consider what to eat and how to go about it. Also, given the alarming statistics discussed earlier, you might want to try a diet plan that doesn't pose any health risk to you and your children. This diet should not exacerbate existing health challenges either, thus making the DASH diet the perfect option.

Introduction

While the focus of this book is on the DASH diet, you will also gain a richer understanding of various foods in general and what we can obtain from them. For instance, you may have heard of good and bad fats but simply knowing that they exist and that you should be careful when consuming bad fats is not enough. You need to know the difference between them and where you can find good fats. These will be revealed to you throughout this book.

This book contains delicious and easy to prepare meals that conform to the DASH guidelines. Whether you need to make breakfast, lunch, or a quick snack for your kids, this book will provide you with diverse and interesting meals. Even better than the health benefits and ease of preparation is the opportunity to strengthen your parent-child bond. This happens as you involve your kids in the cooking process. This time can be spent sharing your culinary knowledge as well as discussing life issues. These moments spent in the kitchen can become so memorable that your kids will draw upon that wisdom for years to come.

I know for a fact that spending quality time with your kids, especially while cooking, is invaluable in building a trustworthy and loving relationship with them. This is because I didn't grow up in such a warm atmosphere. This doesn't mean that my parents never loved me or were always emotionally unavailable. However, love cannot be assumed: little children shouldn't be left to form their own values without proper guidance.

My parents were your typical go-getters who were just too busy to spend quality time in the kitchen with me or sit together at home and enjoy a home-cooked meal. Therefore, we often ate out. Those dispassionate meals cannot be compared to the warmth and connection experienced when you share home-cooked meals (at home) frequently.

The more I grew up and reflected on this, the more I found that this seemingly little problem of not cooking with one's children and eating in can have quite disastrous consequences on both parties: kids and parents. Merely providing shelter, food, education, and other basic necessities for your kids is not enough. You also need to give them love, listen to their concerns, impart knowledge of your experiences, and share good values with them.

Chapter 1: Food as our Foundation

Food is an essential part of our health system because it gives the body all the necessary nutrients needed for proper functioning. Without this, the body's metabolic processes will decline and thus impact our health. However, like a foundation, there shouldn't be too much or too little food—it just has to be the right amount. When food is consumed too little or in excess, it gives the body wrong commands that can lead to health issues, such as obesity, malnourishment, and susceptibility to chronic diseases like heart problems, diabetes, and arthritis. Simply put, health is determined by what one eats.

Food contains nutrients, which are chemicals that empower the cells in the body to carry out their designated duties. In other words, nutrients are nourishments that aid in the maintenance, development, and growth of body functions. Nutrients are essential to health because their absence can cause bodily function to decline. When that happens, health ultimately suffers. However, the availability of nutrients isn't the only problem. As with food, balance is necessary. Nutrients have to be maintained at a specific level to meet our bodily needs. When nutrients fail to meet our required needs, metabolic processes start to decline and may even stop functioning altogether.

Simply put, nutrients direct the body on how to perform, while food serves as a source of information for the body. In this light, we can consider food as a source of nutrients rather than a mass of calories or filling material. We can now focus on building healthy kids with the right mindset and seeing food as building blocks. This way, health is improved, risk of disease decreases, and the body maintains proper functionality.

However, not all foods are good foods. It should come as no surprise that regularly consuming fast food makes for a poor diet, which can affect our waistlines and health in general. According to federal data, over one-third of children and adolescents consume fast food at any one time. Experts reveal that an average of 12.4% of the daily caloric intake comes from consuming fast foods in adolescents and children. Also, children between the ages of 12 and 19 tend to consume up to twice as many calories from fast food as children between the ages of two and 11. In summary, about 34% of adolescents and children between the ages of two and 19 consume fast food on any given day (Sandoval, 2020).

Discrepancies were checked across factors, such as wealth status, weight, and gender, but no changes were recorded. However, further inquiry showed that culture also played a role. In previous studies, reports show that acculturating to the lifestyle of Americans is a key player in adopting unhealthy behaviors like consuming fast food. Focus is on fast food because they're the usual go-to for many but aren't as healthy. High consumption of fast foods leads to unhealthy weight gain and poor quality of dieting in children. To further prove its harmful effects, the CDC posits that the rate of child obesity has more than doubled in children while quadrupling among adolescents across the last thirty years (Centers for Disease Control and Prevention, 2019).

Now, of all the diets you will hear or read about, the DASH diet has proven to be healthier and more effective than the fads that are often advertised. In fact, it was named the best overall diet in 2018 by the U.S. News & World Report and the second-best in 2020. It should come as no surprise that the DASH diet has achieved this level of success since it was developed by accomplished medical professionals, nutritionists, and statisticians in the United States. This also means that while most diets are often best suited for certain age groups or sexes, the DASH diet works f0r everyone effectively.

Dietary Approaches to Stop Hypertension or DASH is not about meal restrictions, nor was it created with weight loss as the objective. Instead, as the name suggests, it was developed in response to the alarming increase in high blood pressure cases. Even teenagers and little kids are frequently diagnosed with high blood pressure. According to the World Health Organization, hypertension is one of the leading causes of early deaths all around the world, and as of 2019, roughly 1.13 billion people in various countries are hypertensive (World Health Organization, 2019).

These numbers are, indeed, disturbing, leading us to appreciate the efforts that went into researching a preventative and curative dietary method for high blood pressure.

However, this diet plan does not only help manage hypertension. As a result of portion control and its characteristic low sodium and low trans fat meals, DASH is also especially effective at helping people healthily lose weight.

One of the biggest reasons people eventually give up on dieting is because they find it difficult to keep up with the extreme meal restrictions and seemingly unsustainable portion sizes of most diet plans. This can be trickier if you are a 9-to-5er or someone who is just too busy to properly consider what to eat and how to go about it. Also, given the alarming statistics discussed earlier, you might want to try a diet plan that doesn't pose any health risk to you and your children. This diet should not exacerbate existing health challenges either, thus making the DASH diet the perfect option.

While the focus of this book is on the DASH diet, you will also gain a richer understanding of various foods in general and what we can obtain from them. For instance, you may have heard of good and bad fats but simply knowing that they exist and that you should be careful when consuming bad fats is not enough. You need to know the difference between them and where you can find good fats. These will be revealed to you throughout this book.

This book contains delicious and easy to prepare meals that conform to the DASH guidelines. Whether you need to make breakfast, lunch, or a quick snack for your kids, this book will provide you with diverse and interesting meals. Even better than the health benefits and ease of preparation is the opportunity to strengthen your parent-child bond. This happens as you involve your kids in the cooking process. This time can be spent sharing your culinary knowledge as well as discussing life issues. These moments spent in the kitchen can become so memorable that your kids will draw upon that wisdom for years to come.

I know for a fact that spending quality time with your kids, especially while cooking, is invaluable in building a trustworthy and loving relationship with them. This is because I didn't grow up in such a warm atmosphere.

This doesn't mean that my parents never loved me or were always emotionally unavailable. However, love cannot be assumed: little children shouldn't be left to form their own values without proper guidance.

My parents were your typical go-getters who were just too busy to spend quality time in the kitchen with me or sit together at home and enjoy a home-cooked meal. Therefore, we often ate out. Those dispassionate meals cannot be compared to the warmth and connection experienced when you share home-cooked meals (at home) frequently.

The more I grew up and reflected on this, the more I found that this seemingly little problem of not cooking with one's children and eating in can have quite disastrous consequences on both parties: kids and parents. Merely providing shelter, food, education, and other basic necessities for your kids is not enough. You also need to give them love, listen to their concerns, impart knowledge of your experiences, and share good values with them. I cook with my own kids now, and I can see how better developed they are than I was at their age. They're confident and energetic children. They're often unafraid to take chances and can be very excited about things that they enjoy. They also treat other kids with love and respect.

Even better than those qualities is the trust they have in me. There is, quite literally, nothing more heartwarming than knowing that your kids can always come to you with their troubles. I want your family to also enjoy this dynamic. Life in today's world can be hectic. However, connecting with your children is ultimately the most important goal, and you need to make time for it. Since cooking with your children is a great way to de-stress, you can make it a weekend ritual.

The DASH meals in this book are not only yummy, healthy, and simple to make, they're also fun. Think of the laughter and stories that will be shared as the main feature, with the sweet-smelling DASH delicacies as a memorable background.

Food is an essential part of our health system because it gives the body all the necessary nutrients needed for proper functioning. Without this, the body's metabolic processes will decline and thus impact our health. However, like a foundation, there shouldn't be too much or too little food—it just has to be the right amount.

When food is consumed too little or in excess, it gives the body wrong commands that can lead to health issues, such as obesity, malnourishment, and susceptibility to chronic diseases like heart problems, diabetes, and arthritis. Simply put, health is determined by what one eats.

Food contains nutrients which are chemicals that empower the cells in the body to carry out their designated duties. In other words, nutrients are nourishments that aid in the maintenance, development, and growth of body functions. Nutrients are essential to health because their absence can fan several aspects of bodily function to decline. When that happens, health ultimately suffers. However, the availability of nutrients isn't the problem alone. As with food, balance is necessary. Nutrients have to be at a specific level to meet the needs of the body. When nutrients fail to meet the required needs, metabolic processes start to dwindle and may even stop.

Put simply, nutrients direct the body on how to perform, while food serves as a source of information for the body. In this light, we can consider food as a source of nutrients rather than a mass of calories or filling material. We can now focus on building healthy kids with the right mindset of seeing food as the building blocks it is. This way, health is improved, diseases are decreased, and the body maintains proper functionality.

However, not all foods are good foods. It should come as no surprise that regularly consuming fast food is poor dieting, which can affect the waistline and health in general. According to federal data, over one-third of children and adolescents consume fast food at any one time. Experts revealed that in adolescents and children, an average of 12.4 percent of the daily caloric intake comes from consuming fast foods. Also, children between the ages of 12 and 19 tend to consume up to twice as many calories from fast food as children between the ages of two and 11. In retrospect, about 34 percent of adolescents and children between the ages of two and 19 consume fast food on any given day (Sandoval, 2020).

The Foundation of Food

Food, in itself, is made up of several building blocks, which play vital roles in wellness. These building blocks are nutrients, which are classified into two groups: macronutrients and micronutrients.

Macronutrients

Macronutrients are nutrients required by the body in large doses, as the term "macro" suggests. Furthermore, the macronutrients' huge requirements stem from the body's inability to provide these nutrients by itself. Also, since we heavily depend on these nutrients for proper body functionality, large amounts are therefore necessary.

Macronutrients provide the body with the raw materials necessary for running the body effectively and are also key to the assimilation and processing of other micronutrients. The human body comprises many mechanisms, both complex and simple in application and uses; this means that many different nutrients are required for optimum functionality. The food that we consume is key in meeting these needs. Macronutrients, in particular, are essential for growth, development, repair, and replacement of damages in the body, energy production, and overall well-being. Each macronutrient has its own function and duty in the body.

Macronutrients typically are made up of three main components in a healthy diet: protein, fat, and carbs. Water comes in as a bonus. While every good food out there is a combination of macronutrients, how much of these macronutrients are available within them makes all the difference. The macronutrient with the highest value in any given food determines the classification of said food. For instance, avocados are made of 2% protein, 8% carbohydrates, and 70% fat. As such, it's classified as fatty food, even though it consists of other macronutrients as well. Alternatively, an apple is made up of 3% fat, 2% protein, and 95% carbohydrates. Hence, it's classified as a carbohydrate. Macronutrients are mostly found in whole foods, such as grains, fruits, vegetables, and legumes, among others.

Types of Macronutrients

1. Carbohydrates: Carbohydrates refer to the fiber, starch, and sugar content found in vegetables, grains, fruits, and milk. Although they are often misaligned in fad diets, carbs are one of the most basic and important nutrients in a healthy diet. As macronutrients, carbohydrates are one of the three main sources of energy for the body. Also, experts believe carbohydrates to be the main source of energy production. The term carbohydrate is derived from the chemical composition of the nutrient, which is a blend of oxygen, hydrogen, and carbon.

Carbohydrates are composed of sugar and starch chains, which are broken down by the body during digestion into glucose. Carbs don't serve the body alone but also are the primary source of energy for the brain. This detail is imperative because the brain constantly requires fuel to function properly. As such, suffice it to say that carbohydrates play a key role in the brain's function and development. Furthermore, in the event of excess glucose, the body converts the nutrients into glycogen, which is stored in the muscles and liver.

Some sources of healthy carbohydrates include:

- Bananas: Bananas are one of the most common fruits across the world. They are classified as carbohydrates because of their nutritional composition of 23% carbs in the form of either sugars or starch. In their unripe state, bananas are high in starch, which changes into natural sugar as bananas ripen, giving it the signature yellow color in the process. Also, the fruit has a high potassium content, a nutrient known to help regulate blood pressure. Additionally, unripe bananas consist of pectin and resistant starch, which are known to aid digestive health.

- Chickpeas: Otherwise called garbanzo beans, chickpeas are one of the staples of the legume family. When cooked, chickpeas have a nutritional value of 8% and 27.4% of fiber and carbohydrates, respectively. While doubling as a good source of carbs, chickpeas also serve as a plant-based protein. Chickpeas contain many minerals and vitamins, such as B-vitamins, phosphorus, and iron. Additionally, chickpeas are linked to improvements in digestive and cardiac health and may also be used to prevent cancer.

- Quinoa: Quinoa is a seed high in nutrients, which has since become popular among natural health enthusiasts. It classifies as a pseudocereal, meaning a seed that is eaten and prepared like a grain. When cooked, quinoa has a carbohydrate content of 22.3 percent, putting it on the high-carb spectrum. Albeit, quinoa also doubles as a rich source of fiber and protein. The seed also contains several other minerals and plant-based compounds that are relevant to health.

Sources have revealed the plant to be helpful in improving blood sugar control. Even better, quinoa has zero gluten content, making it a popular choice instead of wheat for gluten-free dieters. Additionally, its protein and fiber content makes it filling when eaten, so it could also help with weight loss.

- Sweet Potatoes: Sweet potatoes are tuber crops that are as delicious as they are nutritious. When cooked, sweet potatoes have a carbohydrate content of 18 to 21 percent. The carbohydrate content tends to comprise mostly of fiber, sugar, and starch. Asides from providing macronutrients, sweet potatoes also contain potassium, vitamin C, and provitamin A (from beta-carotene). Furthermore, sweet potatoes are rich sources of antioxidants, which have been shown to aid in the reduction of the risk of several diseases as well as oxidative damages.

- Grapefruit: This fruit belongs to the citrus family, which has various flavors such as sweet, sour, and bitter. The fruit has a carbohydrate make-up of 9% and is especially high in multiple minerals, vitamins, and plant-based compounds. Adding grapefruit to your diet can help with insulin resistance and healthy weight loss, making it a great option for people with diabetes. Additionally, due to its nutritional content, grapefruit may reduce cholesterol levels while helping to protect against both colon cancer and kidney stones.

2. Proteins are huge macromolecules made up of one or several other extended chains of amino acid residue. When consumed, proteins have many different functions within the body. They can help with DNA replication, moving molecules from one part of the body to another, in the catalyzing of metabolic reactions, responding to stimuli, and creating structures for cells and organisms. Proteins tend to be different from one another due to a key factor: the sequence of their amino acid formation. This sequence is determined by the nucleotide sequence of the proteins' genes, which results in the transformation of proteins into several 3-D structures. The transformed shapes are the key determiners of their roles in the body.

When it comes to macronutrients, proteins tend to do the heavy lifting in cells, as they're necessary for the creation and retention of structure, regulation, and function in the organs and tissues of the body. Since proteins are basically chains of residues, their basic building blocks are amino acids, which tend to link to other like blocks.

About 20 different forms of amino acids exist, which can be joined to create a protein. It's easy to see proteins in action every other day, as they're responsible for many different functions across the body ranging from storage to enzyme to structural component to antibody to messenger.

Proteins come from two main sources: plants and animals. The body gets most of its amino acid needs from animal-based proteins, such as dairy, eggs, fish, meat, and poultry. However, plant-based sources of protein like nuts, vegetables, beans, and grains are lacking in one or more essential amino acid needs. This doesn't imply that animal-based sources are the only way to go; instead, variety is key. If several plant-based proteins are consumed daily, the body will get all the essential amino acids requirements

Some sources of healthy proteins include:

- Nuts and Seeds: Nuts and seeds are not only good sources of protein, but they also contain healthy ratios of good fiber. They can be introduced into salads or eaten whole as snacks.

- Fish: Many kinds of seafood have high protein content and low levels of saturated fats. Dishes like sablefish (black cod), herring, salmon, anchovies, trout, and sardines have high levels of omega-3 fatty acids. This explains why consuming seafood at least twice weekly is important.

- Soy and Tofu: Soy and non-GMO tofu are among the best alternatives to red meat, which gives up excessive fat but keeps the high protein content. It also helps that plant-based proteins are less expensive than animal-based ones and might be healthier for both your wallet and overall well-being.

3. Dairy products: Dairy products such as yogurt, cheese, and skim milk are a common healthy protein source. Simply avoid low-fat yogurt, which has added sugar, and flavored milk. Also, take a break from processed cheese, which, most often than not, contains non-dairy components.

- 4. Fats: Fats are another macronutrient needed by the body for proper brain development, better absorption of fat-soluble vitamins like A, D, E, and K, and the production of hormones. Of the three macronutrients, fats contain the highest caloric value in a gram, meaning that they need more energy to burn. However, in the same vein, fats help improve feelings of satisfaction, meaning they're more likely to leave you feeling full for longer. For years, fats were considered nutrients to avoid, with many fad diets aiming to abolish fat. The low-fat food crusade began, and the food industry followed the trend. However, this change didn't make any difference. No one was healthier than before, probably because dumping all fats meant leaving out the healthy ones as well. Fat isn't entirely bad because the body needs some of it—the good one, of course. Fat contributes energy to the body and helps with the creation and maintenance of cell membranes—the important exterior of cells and the coating of surrounding nerves.

Fats are also important when dealing with inflammation, muscle movement, and blood clotting. In the long term, certain fats hold more benefits than others; hence the term "good fats." These kinds of fats are usually classified as polyunsaturated and monounsaturated fats. On the other hand, the bad fats are the industrially made trans fats. However, there aren't just good and bad fats; there's also a grey area: saturated fats. Structural-wise, all fats are similar in make, having a chain of bonded carbon and hydrogen atoms. The telling difference lies in the shape and length of the carbon chain, as well as the amount of bonded hydrogen and carbon atoms. These relatively trivial distinctions in the structure translate into many crucial differences in the roles and form of the fats.

Although saturated fats occupy a middle ground in the continuum of good and bad fats, it should be avoided together with trans fats. These fats can be found in processed and packaged foods such as cake mixes, French fries, ramen noodles, and margarine. These fats are bad for the body because they trigger and raise LDL or bad cholesterol levels. On the other hand, they reduce HDL or good cholesterol levels. The unhealthiness of trans and saturated fats stems from hydrogenation, which is a chemical process used in processed and packaged foods to increase shelf life.

Trans fats can be difficult to trace and track, especially on packaged foods, since some laws allow producers to lie about their food content. So, labels reading 0 grams of trans fat may contain some trans fats, but less than 0.5 grams. Unsaturated fats like oleic acid, omega-6, linoleic acid, and omega-3 acids are good fats. Adding these fats to your diet can help with weight loss, proving how counterintuitive the exemption of fat-by-fad diets is. Fat-soluble vitamins such as A, D, E, and K require some form of fat to be absorbed and processed by the body.

Healthy sources of fat include:

- Full-Fat Yogurt: Real yogurts with the full-fat composition are healthy for consumption, as they have all the necessary nutrients comparable to other dairy products with high-fat content. Beyond that, full-fat yogurt is packed with probiotic bacteria, which are healthy and incredibly helpful for overall well-being. According to studies, yogurt can result in key improvements in digestive health and may prove useful in preventing obesity and cardiac problems. Be careful when picking yogurts. Read the labels carefully and ensure you're purchasing the full-fat variety. Sadly, most yogurts found in stores are the low-fat variety but are filled with added sugar. You'll be better off avoiding those.

- Avocados: Avocados are vastly different from other fruits in this category due to their nutritional content. While many fruits are typically loaded with carbohydrates, avocados are rich in fats. Surprisingly, about 77% of the composition of avocados is fat, giving them an even higher fat composition than most animal-based sources. The primary fatty acid in avocados is oleic acid, which is classified as monounsaturated fat. This fatty acid can also be found in olive oil and has been linked with many different health benefits. Furthermore, avocados are rich in potassium, containing up to 40% more than bananas. It doesn't end there, though. Avocados also serve as a great source of fiber and have been proven to help lower triglycerides and LDL cholesterol levels in the body. Alternatively, it improves HDL cholesterol levels.

- Chia Seeds: Although chia seeds aren't generally considered a substantial source of fat, an ounce of it contains about 9 grams of fat, making it a high-fat food. Also, considering that almost every ounce of carbohydrates in chia seeds are actually fiber, the majority of their caloric value comes from their fat content. As a matter of fact, by caloric value, chia seeds are composed of nearly 80% fat. The fats aren't just any type of fats, but ones with good values and healthy outputs like ALA: an omega-3 fatty acid.

- Furthermore, the health benefits of chia seeds are numerous, ranging from decreasing or preventing inflammation to lowering blood pressure. Additionally, chia seeds also contain several other minerals and vitamins, making them a well-rounded food.

- Fatty Fish: Fatty fish is one of the few animal-based sources of fat that is healthy for consumption. Fish such as herring, mackerel, salmon, sardines, and trout are common examples of fatty fish. They are packed with omega-3 fatty acids, which are good for the heart. Additionally, they also have a good protein value made up of high-quality amino acids, as well as other vital nutrients. According to studies, people who eat fish more are more likely to be healthier and have lower risks of dementia, depression, and cardiac problems (Harvard Health Publishing, 2014). Studies have also shown a decrease in susceptibility to many viral diseases. For people who won't or can't eat fish, consider taking fish oil supplements such as cod liver oil. This should help provide the body with all the necessary omega-3 acids needed, as well as vitamin D

Macronutrients

Micronutrient is a term used to classify certain types of minerals and vitamins. Beyond that, the term also extends to various carbohydrates, fats, and proteins required by the body in smaller amounts, hence the term "micro." Since the body is incapable of producing minerals and vitamins by itself, we rely on food for their micronutrient needs. This explains why micronutrients are considered essential to survival. To better understand the concept of micronutrients, you must understand the difference between minerals and vitamins. Minerals refer to inorganic compounds that are found in water or soil and cannot be broken down. On the other hand, vitamins are organic compounds produced from animal and plant-based sources. Unlike minerals, vitamins can be broken down in the presence of air, acid, or heat.

When eating, we consume the minerals that the animals or plants have absorbed, as well as the vitamins they produced. Each food has its own distinct micronutrient content, so consuming a variety of foods to get ample minerals and vitamins is the way to go. Adequate consumption of all necessary micronutrients is imperative for optimal well-being because every mineral and vitamin plays a certain role in the body's maintenance and support.

The importance of minerals and vitamins cannot be overstated, as they are involved in brain development, our growth, and immune functionality, among other vital roles. Depending on their roles in the body, certain nutrients also help prevent and fight against diseases and antibodies.

1. Vitamins: Vitamins are best obtained from food rather than supplements or medicines. So, to get the best value for vitamins, it's best to stick to unprocessed, whole foods. Below are some of the important vitamins required for healthy growth. Keep in mind that the term "vitamins" could also imply minerals.

2. Calcium: Calcium is a vital mineral that is necessary for the well-being of bones and teeth. It can be found in natural sources such as fortified plant-based kinds of milk (like cashew or almond milk) and dairy milk.

3. Vitamin B-12: Vitamin B-12 is an essential vitamin to the body as it acts as a coenzyme in the digestion process, helping to convert food into energy. This vitamin is widely available through injections, liquids, and pills. However, the most effective sources of vitamin B12 are in foods such as eggs, beef, fortified breakfast cereals, fish, and chicken.

4. Vitamin A: Vitamin A is a fat-soluble vitamin that can be found in carrots and other vegetables with similar pigmentation. This vitamin can also be found in meats like liver. Otherwise known as a carotenoid, vitamin A has been shown to improve sight and help in the fight against chronic diseases.

5. Iron: Iron is responsible for the red pigmentation of blood. When you are iron deficient, the body experiences anemia, which has been linked to autoimmune disorders such as lupus. You can obtain iron from foods such as spinach, beans, liver, and clams.

6. Vitamin D: Vitamin D plays a key role in the well-being of the colon and bones. When the skin is exposed to sunlight, the body generates this vitamin. However, the sun can be as beneficial as it is harmful, so experts have found other ways of generating vitamin D3 to prevent deficiency. Foods with high vitamin D content include fatty fish, broccoli, cereals, and egg yolks.

7. Omega-3: Omega-3 fatty acids are one of the healthiest forms of fat that can be found in hemp seeds, algal oil, fish oil, and certain types of fish. Foods with high omega-3 content are known for improving mood, brain function, and cardio vascular health.

8. Vitamin C: Vitamin C is a water-soluble vitamin that is imperative to the immune system and its functions. The vitamin also doubles as an antioxidant, meaning it helps neutralize free radicals, which are believed to trigger the aging of cells. Foods such as red peppers, grapefruit, kale, orange juice, and cherries contain it.

Sources of Vitamins

Fat-Soluble Vitamins:

Sources

Vitamin A   This vitamin can come from foods like fruits and vegetables (mangoes, pumpkins, carrots, and sweet potatoes) and animals (fortified milk, eggs, liver, beef, fish, and shrimp).

Vitamin D   Foods like fatty fish, cereals, and fortified milk are some rich sources of vitamin D.

Vitamin E   Nuts, leafy greens, veggies, vegetable oils, and whole grains help provide the body with vitamin E.

Vitamin K   Vitamin K can come from foods such as kale, broccoli, eggs, cabbages, spinach, and milk.

Water-Soluble Vitamins:

Source

Vitamin B1   Acorn squash, soymilk, ham, and watermelon are rich in vitamin B1.

Vitamin B2   Cereals, grains (whole and enriched variety), milk, cheese, and yogurt.

Vitamin B3   Potatoes, enriched and whole grains, poultry, mushrooms, meat, and fish.

Vitamin B5   Mushrooms, broccoli, chicken, avocados, whole grains, and more.

Vitamin B6   Bananas, legumes, meat, soy products, tofu, poultry, fish, and meat.

Vitamin B7   Fish, whole grains, soybeans, and eggs.

Vitamin B9   Orange juice, broccoli, enriched cereals and grains, spinach, legumes (chickpeas and black-eyed peas), and asparagus.

Vitamin B12   Cereals, cheese, fortified soy milk, meat, fish, and poultry.

Vitamin C Brussels sprouts, bell peppers, citrus fruits (oranges, grapefruits, etc.), strawberries, potatoes, spinach, and tomatoes.

Minerals

Minerals refer to the elements in the earth that are absorbed into foods by plants and animals. They are required by the body for normal growth and functionality. Some essential minerals include selenium, chromium, sodium, magnesium, potassium, manganese, iron, iodine, calcium, phosphorus, fluoride, copper, chloride, and molybdenum.

Chapter 2: Your Role as a Parent

Parenting is a big deal, especially when you try to mold your kids to become healthy. Here, your role goes beyond being a guiding force to becoming a role model and teacher. Kids are inquisitive by nature and impulsive. It would definitely take more than just ordering them around, or worse still: forcing them into it to make them adopt a certain behavior. Understand that change comes by learning and understanding the reason for the process. It isn't enough to lead them down a path. They must understand and be willing to change for themselves.

Make no mistake that adopting a new pattern is no mean feat. So, it's best for the child to be both mentally and physically prepared for the undertaking. Understanding this will help you tune your influence over the family environment, including the types of food they eat and where meals are eaten. The earlier you teach your children about how, when, and what to eat, the more likely they are to continue with healthy eating habits over time: lead the way by walking the talk. Don't be hypocritical about healthy eating habits because your child or children will sooner imitate you than follow the path you try to lead them on.

Also, it doesn't cost much to be a healthy parent yourself. All the many different benefits of foods mentioned in the previous chapter aren't for kids alone. You too can benefit from eating better!

Foods to Avoid

1. White Bread: The majority of bread lining the shelves of commercial outlets are generally harmful to health, particularly when consumed in large amounts. These bread are often made using refined wheat to save cost and have low-fat content. Besides that, they lack in many essential micro and macronutrients and may yet lead to rapid spikes in blood sugar levels. A better alternative to these types of bread is whole-grain bread. While these varieties might be slightly more expensive, they're worth the effort and resources. After all, who can put a price tag on health? For people who are strict on gluten or carbohydrates, you can find other varieties. However, ensure that whole ingredients are used. Alternatively, you could make your own bread and use the ingredients that work best for you.

2. Restaurant Desserts: What's wrong with restaurant desserts? The caloric content per gram, coupled with the unhealthy fat and sugar levels are problematic enough. Then, there's the sodium content that many don't even know or understand. While seemingly harmless, most of these desserts contain way too much salt than necessary. Rather than stuffing yourself full with sodium, try getting a small scoop of sorbet as an alternative. Not only will it help satisfy your sugar craving at the end of a meal, but it's also healthier than most desserts.

3. Deep-Fried Foods: Deep-fried foods are famous for their exquisite flavors and taste. Whether it's fried chicken, chicken fried steak, pork rinds, or fried calamari, chances are you've had one of them before. These foods will rarely ever make it into a healthy meals' menu due to their high levels of calories and fat. Besides that, they also contain alarmingly high amounts of inflammatory AGEs (Advanced Glycation End) products. AGEs are compounds that form when animal-based products are heated at extremely high temperatures for long periods. Continuous exposure to this can result in the gradual erosion of natural defenses, leading to high levels of inflammation and oxidative stress, which are precursors for several diseases. Cutting out foods with high levels of AGEs from your diet, including fried and processed foods, will reduce the chances of inflammation in the body. Grill or bake your foods instead of deep-frying them.

4. Agave Nectar: While the name can be misleading to mean natural and healthy, agave nectar is all but that. It's a sweetener that's often sold as a healthy alternative to many others. Yet, it undergoes a heavy refinement process and comes with high levels of fructose. It's enough of a problem already to have high fructose levels but getting them from added sweeteners is dangerous to your health. As a matter of fact, agave nectar has a higher fructose content than other alternative sweeteners on the market, making it the worst possible choice. In comparison, table sugar is only composed of 50% fructose, and corn syrup (high-fructose variety) has only 55%. It's problematic when even corn syrup seems a healthier alternative than agave nectar, which packs 85% of fructose. Far healthier alternatives to agave nectar are erythritol and stevia, which are both natural and calorie-free.

5. Sweetened Breakfast Cereals: The majority of breakfast cereals are the result of processed grains like corn, oats, wheat, and rice. Cereals are loved by kids and are often chowed down with milk. To make them even more appetizing to the senses, the grains go through a hectic process of flaking, shredding, roasting, pulping, or rolling. At the end of the day, the finished product has unusually high added sugar levels. Without the added sugar—which is the major undoing for these products—cereals may not be as palatable as they appear. In some brands, the added sugar is so high that it rivals candies. However, not all cereals are created equal, so you don't have to give up on them entirely. When buying cereals, go for ones with high fiber content and low added sugars. If you are an oats person, you can skip the process of reading every label and make your own.

There are more unhealthy foods out there than can possibly be covered in this chapter, and you owe it to yourself and your child or children to avoid them. The process doesn't have to have all the fireworks of the fourth of July and can be gradual. Sure, it's a big change, but they can get used to it if you make it the new norm at home. When your kids see you eating healthy, grabbing some chia seeds or carrot sticks instead of hitting the local burger joint, they're more likely to follow in your footsteps. Remember: the goal is not to be exuberant but committed.

Tips and Tricks for Maintaining a HealthyDiet

1. Keep Your Fluid Levels up: It's easy to forget about fluids when talking about healthy eating, but they're just as imperative for good health, especially water. Staying hydrated also helps with avoiding wrong perceptions, like confusing thirst signals to mean hunger. While popular opinions suggest you drink six to eight glasses of liquid a day, it's best if you just stick to regular amounts whenever you feel thirsty. The feeling of thirst is the body signaling a drop in fluid levels, but you don't always have to wait for these signals. As an alternative, you can study the color of your pee to know your fluid level. If you pass a light straw color or plain colorless, you're well hydrated. Otherwise, get something to drink. Although water is the basic and most essential fluid the body needs, you can also try others like coffee, tea, squash (no added sugars), and others. Of course, it's best if you use natural or healthy sweeteners like honey or strawberries for these fluids instead of refined sugar.

2. Learn to Interpret Labels: Reading and understanding food labels is a skill that is undersold in this age and time where many details elude the masses. With this skill, you'll be able to sort out healthy options and avoid unhealthy ones. For instance, you can check for added salt in a can of beans by reading the label. You can also check for the right variety of breakfast cereal to get just by studying it.

3. Don't Go Hungry for Long: A 2016 study on the fluctuations of hormones at different periods throughout a day showed that irregular eating habits negatively affect the metabolism (Paoli et al., 2019). A healthy practice is to be mindful of signs of hunger and fullness and respond accordingly. However, this isn't as easy as it sounds, especially for people who have always ignored these signs over the years. For those people, this is no trivial matter. However, when starting out, it's advisable that you consider spreading out your meals across the day in order to keep blood sugar and energy levels stable. Doing this will also lower the risk of extreme hunger as the day goes by, thus decreasing the likelihood of mindless overeating as well.

4. Focus on the Big Picture Rather Than Tiny Details: Details are necessary, undoubtedly, but shouldn't be prioritized over the big picture. With this knowledge of foods, it can be easy to concentrate on the individual nutrients each food provides, like the number of fats, carbs, minerals, and vitamins or protein in a meal. This is counterintuitive because we eat a wide range of different foods with a mixed bag of nutritional values. So, dispose of the idea of counting macros or micronutrients. Almost all evidence of healthy eating revolves around whole foods and not certain nutrients. An even better approach would be to focus on consuming a variety of healthy foods and focusing on what to expect from them.

5. Balance Is Necessary: The best approach to eating healthy is to combine a huge variety of good, whole foods. However, achieving a balanced diet can also be a great path to combining meals from every essential food group. Below is an outline of the six main classes of foods and the healthy additions you can include in your diet:

- Carbohydrates: To meet your carbs needs, go for couscous, pita bread, whole grains, pasta, quinoa, rice, potato, among others.

- Proteins: For proteins, consider complimentary additions such as eggs, poultry (turkey and chicken), meat, fish, legumes (lentils, chickpeas, and beans), and some cheese.

- Vegetables or salads: As a side dish, consider filling one-third to half of your plate with veggies and salads.

- Fluids: Aim to drink water before, during, and after eating for proper metabolism. Alternative fluids include semi-skimmed milk and sugar-free squash.

- Vitamins and minerals: For your vitamins and minerals needs, aim to consume foods with high calcium content, such as tofu, cheese, dairy alternatives fortified with calcium (oat milk, soya milk, and nuts milk), and yogurt.

Grocery Shopping for Healthy Kids

To get the right foods for yourself and your children, you'll have to unlearn and relearn how to shop for groceries. Now, you can't just stick anything into the basket. You have to be methodical and analyze every food material you pick up. Below is a step-by-step plan to shop for healthy foods.

1. Create a List: It can be easy to slip into impulse buying at the store, so making a list is important before stepping in. You want to make your list before embarking on the journey rather than doing it on-the-go. The former affords you more time to do some thinking and comparisons before arriving at a decision.

2. Go for Low-Fat Varieties: Except with yogurt, it's best to go for low-fat products with foods like gravies, salad dressings, cheese, and milk.

3. Buy Leaner Meat: The labels of packaged meat may be harder to decipher, so it's best to look for the tick of approval from the Heart Foundation. It's also useful to skip the unhealthy parts and go for leaner cuts with fewer fats.

4. Go for Skinned Chicken: The skin on chicken is packed with loads of saturated fats and calories, which are unhealthy. Go for skinned chicken breasts.

5. Be wary of the Salt Content in Processed Foods: Since you may not always be able to decipher the content of processed and prepackaged meats, it's best to limit your consumption of them. Restrict products like chicken loaf, bacon, salami, hot dogs, corned beef, smoked salmon, ham, among others.

6. Only Get Frozen or Fresh Veggies: Vegetables have varying shelf lives, and you don't want anything to do with processed ones. To get the best nutritional value, go for fresh or frozen ones. Pickled and canned varieties should be restricted due to their high salt content.

7. Always Identify the Dates: Every food has a shelf life of its own, hence the best before and production dates on products. These dates help to prevent the risk of consuming harmful perishables, especially those that are frozen over time. A 'Use By' date tells the period within which a product should be consumed, while a 'Best Before' date implies how long until the food loses its best quality.

8. Keep Everything in Their Place: Transporting food home from the market can be a major hassle, especially when it involves high-risk foods such as seafood, dairy products, and meats, which must be kept at certain temperatures. Store these products in their respectable temperatures above 140°F or below 41°F.

9. Don't Turn Down a Bargain: Buying healthy foods in bulk at markets and supermarkets could give you a bargain, so consider this before your next shopping trip. Nonperishable foods with longer shelf lives could come in handy here, some of which include dried pasta, dried veggies, legumes, and beans.

10. Restrict Dependency on Convenient Foods and Takeouts: These foods are costly and have high levels of salt and fat while giving you little to no nutrition in return. Worse still, they'll leave you feeling hungry after only a few hours; they clearly aren't worth your time.

Creating the Perfect Shopping List

1. Organization: Organizing your shopping list is key to effective shopping and saving time and effort. By categorizing your list(s), you can easily go on shopping trips knowing what to get and where to find it. You can categorize your lists according to your chosen pattern, like the layout of the grocery store.

2. Be Realistic in Your Planning: Don't get all caught up and make plans for foods you haven't tried or don't like because you plan to eat healthily. Part of what will make the change easier is enjoying the meal as much as the process. So, only make plans for foods you'll actually eat. It's normal to be excited about trying out new foods or different combinations, but it's best to start with the normal healthy foods you're used to.

3. Make Plans Ahead: Make plans to get all the ingredients required to prepare healthy and tasty meals throughout the week. Not only will this help you eat healthier, but it'll also decrease the risk of considering unhealthy alternatives. With an empty fridge or pantry, you could easily switch to getting takeout or fast food, especially when you are too busy to go shopping. Don't put yourself in the position to slip up, so stock up for the entire week, and be sure to restock when you run out.

4. Keep a Go-to Shopping List: Instead of always scrambling for a pen and paper to draft a shopping list, it's best you always have a running list of items to grab during your trips to the market. You can create the list in a notepad or on your phone: anything that works for you. Just be sure to update the list as you run out of things.

5. Stick to Your List: Keep in mind that grocery shops and marketplaces are designed to upsell you and make you buy unnecessary things on impulse. Whether the products are healthy or not doesn't matter to the sellers. Be sure to avoid the temptation by bringing your list along. Finally, ensure to stick to your list, or, at least, buy all the things on your list first.

6. Try Perimeter Shopping: Perimeter shopping can help with emphasizing the need to purchase healthy foods while minimizing or avoiding contact with unhealthy and processed foods. In most stores and marketplaces, you'll find veggies and fruits in the same aisle as healthy dairy and protein products.

7. Buy Healthy: When creating your shopping list, ensure to add more nourishing and healthy foods. Analyze every item you intend to add and consider if they're a healthy addition to your new lifestyle.

Although it can be challenging at first, especially as it's your first time of mindful planning, you'll get used to it in the long run.

Tips for Leading Healthy Eating Habits as a Parent

1. Have Regular Meal and Snack Times: It's easy to get caught up and forget to eat or put off eating until later. Or, if fad diets have misled you, you now skip meals to avoid weight gain and expend calories. Whatever the case, it's important that you combat these shortcomings in order to become a role model to your kids. Besides that, the change in habits can also help you lead a healthy life.

Contrary to popular beliefs, skipping meals leads to overeating, binge eating, or unhealthy snacking because of the extreme hunger that comes with it. Alternatively, it could result in an unhealthy relationship with food and a cycle that encourages binging. When you eat regularly, you become more susceptible to planning your meals and preparing them. As such, you get to eat more nutritious, well-cooked meals.

Some reasons to eat regularly include:

- Improved Concentration: Focus and concentration tend to wane as time passes when you don't eat regularly. This is because the body lacks the necessary vitamins and minerals to carry out internal processes needed for optimum functionality. Additionally, eating regularly will help you adapt to a healthy routine in which you'll only eat during certain periods.

- Balance: You're more likely to feel in tune and at balance when you eat at the same time every other day, in comparison to how you'd feel with irregular eating habits.

- Minimize Cravings: With the right foods, you are less likely to feel tired and out of your element because your body has all the fuel needed to keep going stronger.

- Nourishment: Usually, the snacks and meals planned for and eaten tend to be healthier and pack the much-needed nutrients for your body to carry out its duties. On the other hand, spontaneous, irregular eating will result in picking meals and snacks out of hunger rather than planning. The meals picked at such points are less likely to be as nutritious as well-planned meals.

2. Eat Together as a Family: Many people have lost mealtimes with family due to over-scheduling and perpetual busyness. Factors like extracurricular activities, school, and work schedules deprive many families of taking the time out to eat together. Some go days, weeks, or months without coming together as a family to eat together and enjoy one another's company. However, this shouldn't be the case. Family meals are vital and should be taken as key parts of day-to-day living. Families that sit together for meals regularly, regardless of what time of day it is, including breakfast, dinner, or lunch, stand to gain many different benefits.

For one, family meals tend to be more nutritious. A study conducted by Harvard University on this subject revealed that families who shared meals are more likely to eat the recommended five servings of veggies and fruits than families who eat separately (Harvard Medical School, 2018). Additionally, children who ate meals with their families were more likely to consume a broader range of foods, and thus, become less picky about food. Beyond eating habits and health, eating together allows family members the opportunity to bond, improve, and build relationships, and strengthen ties. Also, family meals create a sense of belonging that results in an improvement in self-esteem.

At family meals, parents get a chance to be role models to their kids. There, they can set examples of the right table manners and eating habits for kids to follow. Family meals also aid in the prevention of obesity. According to the same Harvard study, people are more likely to eat less when sharing a family meal because they will talk more; thus, eating slowly (Harvard Medical School, 2018). This way, they will quickly notice when they become full rather than rushing through their meals mindlessly.

It might interest you to know that kids who sit to eat with their families have fewer chances of engaging in high-risk habits, such as violence and substance abuse. A family meal could well prevent psychological issues going forward.

3. Don't Pressure Your Child: For many parents, pressuring their children into eating is the way to go, especially when eating their vegetables. However, there are valid reasons to believe that this can have detrimental consequences. Suffice it to say that you can hand a child a veggie, but you can't force them to eat it. A study showed parents who pressure their kids into eating groomed young children into becoming picky eaters (Bailey, 2018). Whether you want your kids to eat faster, slower, or finish their food, it's best to go slowly about it. You don't want to risk making your kids afraid and avoid the process.

A survey carried out on 104 mothers across the United Kingdom with children between the ages of three and five revealed that coercing children into eating significantly contributed to refusals (Salamon, 2011). The children were more likely to dig in their heels and show little to no inclination to eat. The survey further found that avoiding food was a common behavior in children with a particular emotional temperament. This behavior was also found in scenarios where parents used food as a shaping factor for behavior without encouraging a balanced but varied diet. Parents must remember that healthy kids are capable of regulating their fullness and hunger levels.

The survey quoted above further supports other bodies of research that showed that when caregivers and parents override the signals of fullness and hunger given by their kids by pressuring the kids into eating, the children are likely to struggle with appropriately regulating their appetite going forward. It gets worse if the kids are fussy eaters, as pressuring them into eating can lead to more conflicts and problems during mealtimes. When asked, these mothers rated some of the many different behaviors exuded by their kids during mealtimes. They reported under-eating as a way of expressing emotional states, food fussiness, and slowness in eating, including how easily kids asserted to be full.

4. Stock up on Healthy Alternatives: You don't have to be perfect to eat healthily. Even at 80 percent, you'll be doing a fine job of it. The idea is to make an effort, no matter how little. Even the littlest change in the right direction counts. However, all your efforts can easily come to nothing if you fail to plan for contingencies. You will most likely run out of good, healthy foods and snacks at some point, and those periods can be dicey. With some main staples on your shelves, you can easily whip up a meal or snack much faster than it'd take the delivery guy to arrive. Not only will your body and mind be healthier, but you'll be fuller for longer, and would have saved on resources. Below are some healthy alternatives to stock up on:

a. Canned Tuna: Many people fail to consume enough omega-3 fatty acids; where better to find this helpful fat than in fish? While seemingly common to get, not all fish are healthy. So, you want to go for an easily-available and pocket-friendly alternative like tuna.

Fresh tuna may be on the pricey side, so you could easily get the canned variety, which has similar health benefits to the former. However, it's best to go for the tuna in water variety, which has lower caloric value while packing more vitamin D and protein. It helps that tuna is a versatile food that can be made in several ways, such as tuna casserole, tuna salad, and tuna burgers or patties.

b. Eggs: Eggs are another common, versatile food that serves as a good alternative to big breakfasts. They can be eaten whole, in a burrito, or in a frittata. For lunch ideas, you can always try a trusty egg salad. The protein content in eggs, which is up to 7g per egg, can help in controlling hunger and leaving you feeling fuller for longer. Hence, you are less likely to crave high-calorie foods as the day goes by. Additionally, egg yolk is rich in choline, which helps to improve mental health.

c. Canned Beans: Canned beans are a great source of macronutrients, packing healthy carbohydrates and proteins. They can be added to soups and salads and are especially great to taste. They can easily replace fish or chicken in some meals and are just as filling. However, not all canned beans are healthy.

Ensure to study their labels and avoid ones with MSG. Also, during preparation, make sure that they are properly rinsed and no longer feel sudsy to the touch. The brine the beans sit in can lead to bloating and gassing after consumption. Black beans are especially great in this category. About half a cup of black beans has as much fiber as two pieces of whole-wheat bread and as much protein as a whole egg. You can experiment with black beans, as there are several recipes to pick from, such as black bean brownies, black bean burgers, and black bean salad with cilantro, vinegar, peppers, corn, olive oil, and tomatoes.

d. Canned Soups: Another packaged alternative food to have at home is canned soups. The low sodium variety with organic packaging is the way to go for making healthy snacks or meals easily. However, watch out for preservatives when making your pick. Also, make no mistake about the vegetable content, as they may not be the freshest around, but they'll be good in case of an emergency and are healthy too. Go for canned soups with many grains and vegetables but steer clear of those without cream bases. Some healthy varieties to consider are wild rice soup, chicken soup, vegetable soup, and bean soup.

e. Granola: Granola is one of those foods which can be healthy alternatives until they are ruined by added sugar. But, if you avoid those with artificial sweetening (low-sugar variety), granolas are healthy for consumption. They are made with seeds, nuts, and grains, which are guaranteed to keep you going for longer. To get granola with low sugar content, study the labeling. Ensure that the one you settle for doesn't have sugar high in the ingredients list. The only other sweeteners acceptable in healthy granolas are maple syrup and honey.

f. Tomato Pasta Sauce: This food is easy to prepare and very healthy. All you need to do is sauté the pasta sauce with any healthy meat (ground) and throw in some pasta if you want. Voila: you have a meal! However, don't just take every tomato pasta sauce at face value. Study the label and look out for any additives. Only settle for ones with whole foods and nothing more. Tomato pasta sauces are packed with antioxidants like lycopene and vitamin C.

The Don'ts of Being a Model Parent

1. Keeping Children Out of Kitchens: It's understandable that you don't want your kids to get hurt when you're preparing a meal. The kitchen is like a battleground with sharp knives, hot stuff, and choking hazards. However, keeping your children away from the kitchen can be a bad idea. According to studies, engaging kids in the process is a great first step in making them try new dishes (Curran, 2019). When children are involved in the process of preparing their meals, there's some part of them that wants to try what they've made. Radishes are the devil for most kids, but studies show that when kids are allowed to cut up these vegetables and make some salads, their tastes change. Suddenly, they think radishes aren't so bad after all.

2. Don't Keep Out of Reach of Children: Restricting your kids from the good stuff isn't a path to redemption. It's normal for parents to worry that their children may binge on unhealthy treats, so they resort to keeping these foods out of reach and sight. Another study on the same subject revealed that kids in a household with many restrictions on food were more likely to resort to binging, especially when they happen on restricted foods away from home. The lesson here for parents isn't to stop restricting certain foods but to do away with the ideology altogether. If you must restrict food, don't stock it. It's best to not set up a system that causes your kids to slip up. Instead, stock your homes with healthy snacks, which the kids can easily access whenever they want.

3. Giving up Easily: Everyone has their limits, and sometimes, kids push parents beyond theirs. Hence, why some parents give up outright. You'll typically hear such parents say, "my kid wouldn't eat this or that." Although that may be true here and now, there are health risks involved like allergies; also, eating preferences tend to evolve as a child grows. So, as a parent, it helps to keep your options open and not see a child's unwillingness or reluctance as the final straw. Continue preparing several varieties of healthy foods and serving them to your children, even if the child never takes a bite out of the meal. For younger kids, it could take about 10 attempts or more across a king period of time to notice and try the food. Other factors that could influence a child's eating habits are friendships and sibling dynamics. Kids are likely to build their eating habits around people that resonate well with them.

4. Going on a Diet: Children are easily influenced by their parents' eating habits and preferences. As such, they are more likely to consume the foods that they see their parents eating regularly. A study by Rutgers on the food preferences between parents and children revealed that preschoolers tended to reject or like the same foods as their parents (Parker-Pope, 2008). In other studies, it was revealed that girls have a higher chance of picking at their meals if their mothers hate veggies. Considering this, suffice it to say that parents should be more aware of how dieting habits influence their kids. A child's perception of healthy eating and food, in general, could be ruined by the dieting routine of their parents. In a study carried out on girls aged five, a kid believed that dieting revolved around drinking chocolate milkshakes, and closer inquiries revealed that her mother took Slim-Fast drinks regularly (Abramovitz & Birch, 2000). For another child, dieting meant cooking food but not eating it.

The Dos of Model Parenting

The bane of encouraging healthy eating habits is to keep serving children several nutritious foods and alternatives. Beyond that, here are some tips you could also try:

1. Allow Kids Some Independence: Children typically start finger-feeding as they approach nine months of age and will usually make the leap to utensils around their first and second birthdays. As parents, you must ensure that there is enough for your child to eat so that they don't get frustrated. As much as necessary, try to help them eat, but don't get carried away and ignore signs of satisfaction or other hunger cues. Remember, you can always give the child more food if they want, but you can't take back what you overfeed them. When feeding your child, you'll likely feel urged to get the child to eat yet another bite. This urge might resurface when the child starts to eat on their own. Resist the urge and let your child do as they see fit. Many parents wrongly believe that it's best not to let kids feed themselves, especially in their younger years. However, this is wrong as it deprives kids of their right to control. They have to decide how, what, and whether or not to eat—for this is the process through which they learn their tastes and understand internal cues of hunger and satisfaction. Also, younger kids must learn to be independent when eating.

2.Only Serve Correct Portions: Many parents tend to overestimate the amount of food a child can eat, especially when they fancy the food. Serving kids a couple of tablespoons could be too much. Start by serving small portions, which are altogether less overwhelming. This way, they can ask for second helpings if they're not full yet. However, with large portions, children may feel pressured to eat and may learn to overeat as a result.

3. Refrain From Negotiating Meals: Encouraging children to take a bite of their meals is no biggie, but don't mistake that to be the same as negotiating bites. When punishments or rewards are attached to meals, negotiation sets in. Your job is to provide them with healthy meals, and that's about it. It's up to the child to decide their eating behaviors.

4. Understand Your Child: Kids tend to express their growing independence through eating habits, explaining their choice to eat or not eat. As such, it's only natural that some kids will turn out as picky eaters with or without external influences. If they don't fancy a certain type of food, they'll skip it and that's about it. If they fancy one food, they might be on about it for a long time. Then, some parents might feel the child is stuck on the said food and try forcing the child into trying other meals. This is wrong, as the child may get tired of the food soon enough to turn their attention elsewhere. If the favorite food phase seems to be lasting forever, you can try adding new foods to their meals. That way, you've introduced variety into their mealtimes without depriving them of what they're willing to eat. Continue doing so until they start to take interest in the other foods, then you can switch their meals.

5. Plan and Have Family Meals: Ensure that your child has their own place at the family's dinner table. It helps when kids grow up sharing meals with their siblings and parents. It also helps to kickstart and maintain the culture of eating healthy foods. Your child will be more inclined to eat their veggies and fruits when they share family meals.

6. Pay Attention to Your Child: Pay attention to the verbal and nonverbal cues given off by your kids. A child that picks out onions from their meals could be indicating that they're not a fan of it. It could also be an indication that they don't enjoy the meal or are full. Forcing the child to eat regardless of their actions may teach them to ignore vital cues that help them understand how and when to eat or stop eating. This doesn't mean that it's practical or advisable for kids to eat on demand all day long. Those who eat all day may not learn what it's like to be hungry or full. That's why structured meals and snack times are important.

Kids can manage their hunger when they come to expect that food will be available during certain times of the day. If a child chooses not to eat anything at all, simply offer food again at the next meal or snack time.

Create positive peer pressure. Toddlers are more likely to eat fruits and vegetables if they see their peers eating them, so look for opportunities where they can eat healthy with friends.

Chapter 3: Letting Them Be The Chef

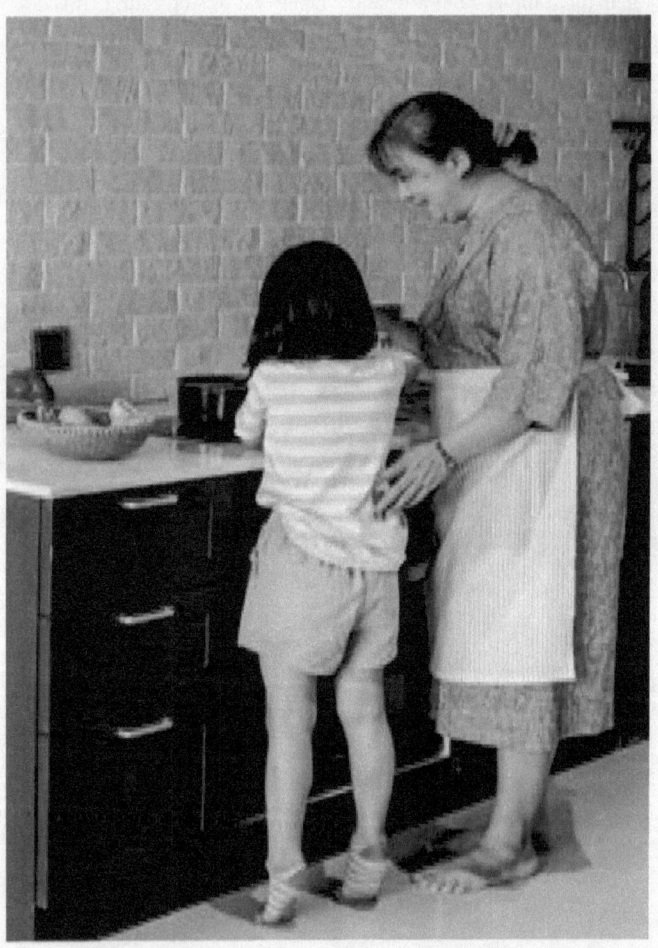

The art of a whole family cooking, including grandparents, parents, and children, exchanging family secrets and recipes passed down through generations is one that's lost to time across many households in the world.

In recent times, parents are too busy to bother teaching their kids basic cooking skills, and grandparents often live too far to be of any help. It's such a sad reality. Make no mistake, inciting your kids to cook isn't nearly as easy as it sounds. It requires a great deal of patience, good temperament, and enough time for cleaning up. This is especially the case when dealing with younger kids. Nonetheless, for all it's worth, it's an art that is best rediscovered.

The possibilities are endless. Cooking with your children helps to get them involved and interested in the healthiness of what they consume and their well-being in general. It also helps them to take interest in foods they'll normally be disinclined to try. Sure, kids will always be kids: enjoying snacking on unhealthy chips they're offered at a school party or chugging down Kool-Aid after a soccer game. However, the key thing is how and what they eat the majority of the time. That major part is where you form in as a parent: where your influence can be most felt. Bear in mind that many kids today have the wrong perception of eating healthy. For them, getting in some veggies and fruits, as well as some legumes and whole grains from time to time should help. The pickier of them will pick leaner varieties of animal-based foods and some fish when they feel like it. Truly, this knowledge is substantial enough, but more can be done.

Bringing your child to cook with you doesn't encourage them to eat healthy alone. There are many more benefits than meets the eye, some of which were recommended in a report on obesity in children and teens (Government of Canada, 2019). Some of these benefits include the following:

1. It involves children in the process of planning, getting, and preparing healthy meals: skills that would be useful in both long and short terms.

2. It reduces the amount of meals they consume outside because they're less likely to get hungry easily or find unhealthy alternatives.

3. It teaches them about structure and the effects of family meals on health.
Indeed, cooking with your children is a gift that never stops giving with vital payoffs going forward.

How to Engage Your Children in Cooking

A good starting point would be the first meal of the day: breakfast. Evidence shows that eating breakfast helps to improve mental health. This is especially so when breakfast meals are healthy and rich in nutrients and fiber coming from dairy, fruits, and whole grains. It'd be unwise not to consider the fact that parents could be pressed for time during the early hours of the day. To compensate for this, you could take out the time during weekends, on school holidays, or on family vacations to cook with your kids. If that doesn't work still, consider dinner.

Dinner works best for some parents because it's when they're done with their commitments and only have to focus on making meals. To make the experience fluid and comfortable, you can take out some vegetables and fruits and cut them up as snacks to eat on the go. You could also get beverages (zero calories variety) to sip on. With these in place, the kids are less likely to be hungry and eat the dinner ingredients as they cook.

Now, to the more obvious question of age. How old do kids have to be to indulge in cooking or help out? Largely, there is no template or fixed time for such engagements. Some kids tend to be more interested in cooking from their younger years, say two or three, and that isn't a bad time to start.

Tips for Dealing With Kids Under Age Five

These kids can be given small tasks like:

1. Snapping, tearing, scrubbing, breaking, and dipping (For instance, you can make them scrub
the pots while you do the dishes)

2. Using a biscuit or cookie cutter to cut, spread, and shake

3. Removing corn husks

4. Washing vegetables and draining in a colander

5. Mashing, juicing, filling, and peeling some food items

6. Measuring and pouring certain ingredients

7. Mixing ingredients by hand

Dealing With Kids Above Eight

Children above the age of eight but below teenage years are much older and can handle more advanced tasks than the previous category. You can give them tasks like:

1. Stirring food over the stove under adult supervision

2. Reading recipes and gathering ingredients on their own

3. Operating a food processor or can opener with safety measures in place

4. Cracking and separating eggs

5. Grating cheese and vegetables

6. Creating recipes for easy meals and snacks

7. Using an electric mixer under adult supervision, if necessary

8. Operating and analyzing a candy thermometer under adult supervision

9. Using dinner or plastic knives to cut up fruits and vegetables

Making The Most of Family Time

Cooking and sharing meals as a family can be difficult to achieve, but it's absolutely worth the time and effort. If everyone is involved and willing to help, the family will more likely share more mealtimes and cook together. When kids come of age, it's important to begin easing them into the process of planning, sourcing for, and preparing healthy foods. These skills are important to life and well-being and will greatly impact them.

Start small when introducing children to helping out in the kitchen. You can get them started on small tasks like taking out food from the cupboard or fridge, washing veggies and fruits, tearing up lettuce for salads, lining pans with muffin liners, or sprinkling grated cheese on pizza.

Kids who have more experience helping out in the kitchen should help other kids ease into the new role. They can teach them how to do little tasks, while you focus on doing other things. Children will most likely eat the foods they helped to prepare, and this will eliminate the need to pressure them to eat.

Cooking as a family could be a great way to bond, indulge each other, and have some quality fun time as a family. Teach children to use fresh ingredients and already prepared foods around them to easily whip up new meals. As time goes on, teach them to make meals from scratch. Remember, their first attempt doesn't have to be Gordon Ramsay-esque. What matters is the time you spent together and the skills they picked up during the process.

Who said cooking is the only thing that happens in a kitchen? When cooking together, you can teach your children about hygiene and food safety. Teach them to wash their hands before and after cooking and eating. Also, help them understand why it's important to wash fruits and vegetables before eating. While you're at it, teach them to differentiate and separate ready-to-eat meals and those that need cooking.

A lesson on kitchen safety isn't less appropriate at this time, either. Endeavor to keep an eye on your kids while in the kitchen with them. All the fun can easily go down the drain when someone gets a cut or burn.

If you don't feel confident about your cooking skills, don't go overboard. Instead, settle for recipes that are easy to make and familiar to all. Not only will you enjoy the time spent with your kids, but you'll save considerable time and efforts that would have gone into deciphering a complex recipe.

It's not enough to cook with your kids alone. You have to go all the way. So, what's next after cooking? Enjoying the meal together.

When you share the meal you prepared with your kids, you have even more time to bond. This will evoke a sense of security, safety, and love with your kids.

Mealtime is a good time to enjoy each other's company instead of focusing on how a child eats or what they prefer. Don't ruin the moment.

You can teach children about nutrients and health during mealtimes, citing the foods being eaten at the moment as ample examples.

Only start and continue positive conversations around the table. This will allow for better communication with your kids, ensuring that you understand what's going on with them. Leave our disciplinary or cautionary conversations for another time. The table is for enjoying the meal, talking about good foods, and bonding.
Turn off or keep out distracting items like phones, tablets, computers, and TVs at the table. Books and toys should be off-limits as well.

Beyond nutrition and health, cooking can also be a good way to teach your children about other subjects learned at school. Matter of factly, it could be a more hands-on approach with huge potential, as the teachings will involve physical materials. Thus, evoking their sense of calculation and focus. With cooking, you can improve the math skills of your kids, brush up on their science and reading skills, and teach them life skills. Unlike classwork, the lessons in the kitchen are fun, with tasty and nourishing rewards to urge them on.

Younger kids may not be entirely ready to decipher and comprehend the math and chemistry of cooking; however, watching and engaging in the process can pique their curiosity and enhance learning. Children can be taught basic chemistry when mixing ingredients, stirring, and seeing the effects of the heat in food items. While it might appear trivial, the presence of these learning opportunities around them—and at a basic and more understandable level—is a gift that truly ages well.

For older kids and adults, basic math (multiplication, subtraction, addition, and division) may not matter, but it'd mean a lot to younger kids to see the real-world applications of things that are taught at school. In this light, it's important that you take out the time once a week, at least, to indulge your kids in the kitchen and teach them some basic skills. Make no mistake, the process is demanding and requires lots of planning and selecting recipes, but it's a worthwhile endeavor. Below are some cooking ideas your kids can learn from:

1. Colors: They are everywhere around us. What makes cooking an ideal learning experience is the fact that colors are imperative to the process. We know meat is done when it turns brown, and rice becomes even whiter when cooked. The best way to learn about colors would be with fruit salads. Now, the lesson plan can be used in two ways. Suppose your kids are on the younger side, and approaching the initial stages of language acquisition, in this case this food is perfect because the colors of the salad pop and are less likely to be easily forgotten. However, older kids are not to be left out, because this salad has enough for everyone. You could engage them in cutting up the fruits and vegetables and sharpen their cooking skills. Children who take foreign language courses are likely to have already a list of vocabulary-building words consisting of foods and colors, which are some of the first lessons.

You can learn these words yourself and teach your children to form simple sentences. For instance, "Strawberries are red, and grapes are green." Doing this, not only do you nail down a lesson on colors, but you also help improve their fluency.

2. Patterns: Children who loved Ratatouille, a cartoon by Disney, will no doubt enjoy the process of creating a similarly layered vegetable tian. This food is a great way to teach younger kids about patterns. To avoid injuries, only serve them pre-sliced vegetables and watch them create different patterns and alternate between colors. Encourage them to repeat several patterns and guess the next vegetable to be added.

3. Weights: What better way to learn about weights than with pound cake? This dessert gets its name from the number of ingredients used to prepare it, one pound of butter, flour, eggs, and sugar each. The classic recipe for pound cakes, drafted with the volumetric measurements, can help kids explore proportions. Furthermore, they will also be exposed to the concept of weight, as different substances will likely weigh differently. You can begin with the popular riddle: what weighs more, a pound of cement or a pound of feathers? As they get exposed to weights in the long run, introduce them to how weights are measured and allow them to use the kitchen scale. In time, they'll understand the concept behind the dessert's name and learn valuable lessons about weights.

4. Alphabetizing: Cobb salad is a dish made with layers of many different ingredients such as tomatoes, eggs, bacon, and cheese. The ingredients are arranged in different lines across a layer of lettuce. When making this dish with your kids, allow them to help in assembling the ingredients. That way, you can teach them to alphabetize by showing them the alphabetical ordering of the different ingredients.

5. Oxidation: Chemistry can be a hard subject if the basics are not understood. With guacamole, you can help your child understand the basics of oxidation. With a wide range of fruits such as bananas or apples that turn brown in a couple of minutes or hours when cut, a lesson is prepared. While preparing a guacamole recipe, you can explain that the browning effect is the way these fruits protect themselves from the dangers of oxygen. You can further experiment with the addition of acids from lime and tomato on your avocados to retain their bright green color when the meal is prepared.

6. Fermentation and Yeast Action: Pizza is a popular food across the world and can even teach a lesson. However, the lesson here can't regularly be taught like the others on this list as pizza is a tedious dish. Preparing the dough can be a fun and tactile activity for kids of any age group. Pick a pizza recipe of your choice and use it to teach your kids about the cheese's action on the dough. Go further and teach them about the pros and cons of consuming sugar as you create ring pockets of air that will surface in the end product. While you're at it, feel free to throw in a lecture on baking, like kneading and how gluten strands form to strengthen the dough's structure. Round up the lecture by allowing your kids to have fun by adding any toppings of their choice to their pizzas.

7. Centrifugal Force: Physics is even more fun when you engage in practical activities. With a simple egg salad recipe, you can introduce your children to the concept of the centrifugal force. It'll give them the chance for them to see this force in action. Grab a raw egg and spin, watching as it slows to a stop easily. Get a hard-boiled egg and repeat the spin. Watch how it spins for longer before stopping. This little visual already captures the essence of centrifugal force and how it works. This is an experiment to perform before you start preparing the salad with the hard-boiled eggs.

8. Fractions: At every level of education, everyone deals with one sort of fraction or the other, so this lesson is always a good one. With vinaigrettes—a tasty topping used on salads—you can easily impart the knowledge of fractions. Vinaigrettes can be used to show proportions and fractions in a more hands-on approach than most meals. Pick a vinaigrette recipe of your choice and show your kids how to measure items using tablespoon measures and measuring cups. You can ask your older kids to double or halve the recipe to engage them in the skills they have learned.

9. Geometry: Geometry is the study of shapes and a phenomenon that exists all around us. In the kitchen, the possibilities of teaching geometry are almost endless. Cookie dough is cut into different shapes and sizes such as circles, rectangles, or triangles. Which shape or size results in the most cookies? Do all cookies have the same size? Children are better able to decipher and comprehend how sheets of dough of similar sizes can be cut up into individual pieces using any recipe of your choice.

10. Chemical Reactions: Chemical reactions are as wild as they come, as you'll see in crazy cakes. Most cakes have eggs and baking powder in their recipes as leavening, but not crazy cake: this dessert uses baking soda and vinegar instead. When making the recipe, explain to your kids that the combination of vinegar makes the cake rise. You can make a trial run where you make a bit of the cake without vinegar to show them the difference.

Building a Family Culture Around Cooking

Family and food are inseparable from culture. In many cultures worldwide, especially in Africa, food is eaten more than to satisfy hunger. It also serves cultural purposes. In this light, it's understandable why some cultures are particular about food and attach importance to them. Beyond cultural roles, many cultures prize mealtimes with friends and family. With the rise of globalization and industrialization, the world as we know it is evolving. Restaurants and eating out spots pop up across the globe regularly. The increase in the number of hotels worldwide can be linked to the surge in demand for takeout.

With the ease of finding food that comes from globalization, many people now dread the process of cooking, preferring to eat at restaurants or get processed and pre-packaged foods. The usual excuse for the bulk of them is exhaustion from work, eating for cheaper outside the home, lack of time, and other reasons. However, it's shocking to note that a growing number of young people admittedly don't know how to cook. Among this lot, the culture of home-cooked meals has been relegated to the background in favor of other alternatives. In a study conducted by the CDC, men are shown to have a higher inclination to consume fast foods than women (Fryar et al., 2018). A whopping 46.5% of males between the ages of 20 and 39 are huge visitors to restaurants.

In comparison, takeouts and restaurant meals aren't nearly as healthy as home-cooked ones. Many people have argued that the latter will continuously trump the former for many obvious reasons. For one, restaurants prepare generic meals for all audiences but don't take the health or nutritional requirements of everyone into consideration. On the other hand, a home-cooked meal is prepared with the eater in mind. Aside from that, homemade food tends to be more organic as you're in full control of the ingredients you use. Restaurants, however, use ingredients that help them save costs the most. Additionally, homemade meals are less likely to have adverse effects on your health in comparison to takeouts, which contain insane levels of salt, chemical additives, and sugar.

Focusing on the health benefits of home-cooked meals alone will undermine other advantages that come with cooking your meals. Below are several reasons why retaining a healthy kitchen culture is beneficial to both your health and that of your kids:

1. Control: You can only control the things that are within your grasp, but all of that changes with outside foods. Controlling how food is made and served is the first step to a healthy life—a chance you can only get by opting for homemade meals. If you are particular about your kids' weights, want to prevent the prospect of an allergic reaction, or follow a special medical regimen, you'll have to cook your own meals. When preparing your meals, you're in control of how much sugar, salt, and fat goes into the food. When it's all done and ready for eating, you still control the sizes of each serving. These are rights you don't get with eating outside your home.

2. Improve Creativity: Preparing homemade meals means you're entitled to altering recipes to suit your taste. When you aren't doing that, you can simply experiment with a recipe and try different ways of spicing things up. You don't know what you like until you try making it.

3. Combats Depression: There are activities that help people take the edge off and reach that point of zen. Cooking is one of such activities that can be therapeutic to some people. When cooking, attention isn't readily diverted to other problems or distractions around you. The mind will then fully concentrate on the task before it, thus reducing anxiety over other things in the long run.

In summary, cooking shouldn't be considered as a daunting process. It's not rocket science and is as easy or as complex as you imagine it to be. If you are a beginner, start easy and go for simple dishes. You can start with making a meal or two twice daily. Repeat recipes regularly to get the hang of it. Using work or other activities as an excuse to shy away from cooking is unhealthy in the long run. Eating healthy is good business, and it lies in your hands to make it work. Consider making food in large quantities to last the week. Prepare your favorite cuisines and snacks to eat as you go, so you don't have to stress about what to eat regularly. Also, try your best possible to ensure you don't put your time and effort into meals you don't like. You'd only be creating unnecessary pressure for yourself, which is a far cry from the purpose of a healthy kitchen culture.

Kitchen Safety

During the holidays, your kids could be bored out of their minds wondering how to spend time. Aside from being fun and a bonding experience, you can indulge your kids in the kitchen. However, before making cute chefs out of your offspring, it's best if you teach them about safety and hygiene in the kitchen first. Not only will you be equipping them with life skills, but they'll also get a sense of maturity and independence from learning to take care of themselves in the kitchen.

Over time, as they sharpen their kitchen skills, they could become good cooks and make healthy foods for the family. Kitchen safety isn't a subject for older kids alone. Preschoolers and toddlers are also eager to

help out, so they shouldn't be dismissed either. The subject of personal safety depends on the extent of help required, the age and maturity of the helper, previous kitchen experience(s), and the tools or equipment involved.

Supervision would be needed depending on how young or inexperienced the child is. However, even older kids could sometimes do with some supervision. It wouldn't hurt for the adult to ensure safety precautions are in place, especially when harmful objects, such as stoves, ovens, and knives, are used.

Safety for Baby Chefs

Cooking with younger children can be either fun or a disaster, depending on how well you manage the situation. Little kids being eager to please won't mind holding ingredients and fetching items. They can also help with pouring, shaping, measuring, portioning, or pushing buttons on food processors, mixers, or blenders. They can help to rinse and drain vegetables and fruits before use. Older and more experienced kids tend to feel more mature when supervising and helping out younger kids. That's one way to ensure your babies are safe while doing their bit to help with cooking.

On your part, ensure that the work surfaces used by younger kids are at appropriate heights for the size and height of the child. If a chair or stool must be used, ensure to only set up ones that are sturdy and well-balanced: you want to avoid the risk of wobbling and falls. On other surfaces such as stovetops and countertops with knives and other injurious tools, you might not want to take the gamble. If you must, be there to hold and supervise them.

General Safety and Hygiene

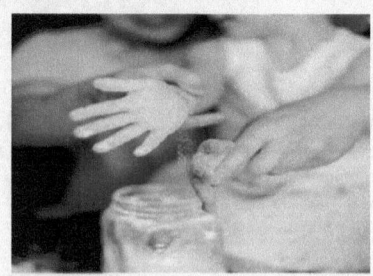

For kids of all ages, certain basic discussions should be had before embarking on a cooking project. Your first go-to should be to stress the importance of cleaning their hands. It's important to wash the hands before beginning the process, and during, especially when you have to handle materials like seafood, raw meat, raw eggs, and poultry. Furthermore, you need to nail down rules on tasting recipes, such as pancake batter and quick bread, which contain the previously mentioned items. As the leader, groom your children to make a habit of cleaning up their worktops regularly and tidying the kitchen after cooking is done.

Another safety education that cuts across all ages and sizes is knife safety. Review and discuss knife safety with your kids regularly. There are many materials online on how to handle knives and the type of knives to use at any one time. Learning from these materials and teaching your kids will further improve their safety with knives. For younger kids or children with less kitchen experience, you could get them started with blunt knives. However, this tactic can backfire if you don't understand how it works. Blunt knives require more effort to cut things, thus improving the chances of an accident.

To prevent this, ensure that blunt knives are only used to cut soft foods. Alternatively, you can get sturdy, serrated knives made of plastic. You could also get knife guards, which are held with non-dominant hands to ensure that foods are safely cut. Also, you should never forget to remind your kids to never drop sharp knives into soapy water used to wash dishes; accidents could happen with slippery knives.

Oven and stove safety is another important discussion that should be had with your kids. Always have oven mitts on hand as a reminder for kids to use them. Also, emphasize the importance of turning off appliances after cooking.

Practicing With Kid-Friendly Recipes

The recipes you select for your kids to make should be appropriate for their level of experience and age. The best, kid-friendly recipes are always baked goods because they don't always require the use of sharp equipment, and cooking is done away from reach.

Foods like soft pretzels, pancake or waffle batter, scones, yeast rolls or bread, muffins, and quick bread are a hit.

You can also try single dish meals, such as egg meals (crustless quiche, omelets, and scrambled eggs), stir fry, stuffed shells, veggie pizza on whole-grain dough, and pasta dishes. You could also try to make quesadillas, tacos, and burritos. Kids could have some fun with shaping foods such as turkey burgers and meatballs. You can also indulge them in mashing up ingredients for hummus and guacamole to eat with raw vegetables. Another kid-friendly recipe that encourages the consumption of vegetables is kale chips.

Kids of all ages can be indulged in preparing meals like wraps, pita pockets, and sandwiches. Young kids who like using cookie cutters could be allowed to cut their sandwiches into fun shapes. Additionally, you can use cookie cutters to make egg-in-a-hole, which is a meal prepared using bread. Cut any shape into the middle of a bread slice and place on a well-oiled nonstick pan. Add scrambled egg or raw egg into the cutout and cook the bread on both sides until the egg is cooked to your desired taste.

The process of making California rolls is fun, because it promises several activities for kids, ranging from the preparation of the ingredients to making the rolls. You can also encourage your kids to create their own special smoothie recipe in a blender using the vegetables and fruits of their choice. Alternatively, you can encourage them to make granola or any other personalized healthy mix, which you can add to a fruit parfait or yogurt as a healthy dessert.

Tips for Cooking With Kids

1. Teach Them to Touch and Taste: Teaching your kids to touch and taste foods and food items will obviously make the process an enjoyable one for them; in turn, this encourages them to be more adventurous and increase their palate. Additionally, it's a good way to teach the kids the foods that can be consumed raw without any consequences. Teach them to taste with a clean spoon rather than with the cooking spoon or their fingers.

2. Consider the Ability and Age of the Child Involved: The majority of kid-friendly recipes come with age guidelines. However, you know your child best. You know your child's capability the most and are better suited to picking the recipes that best suits their abilities. There are activities for almost all age groups, even if all they have to do is splash their hands in the sink and pretend to be washing veggies and fruits. Older kids can deal with more complex tasks like chopping items and cooking.

3. Always Plan Ahead: Pick a recipe that's appropriate for your kids, one that involves various activities for everyone, and is suitable for their ages. It will be enjoyed in the end. Ensure that you have all the tools and ingredients necessary to make the meal. If possible, start preparing the kitchen before inviting your kids to join you. For instance, baking is fun for everyone, but you might want to start preheating the oven, laying out the materials, and categorizing tasks before bringing your kids in.

4. Prepare your Kids: It's not enough to be prepared yourself: you also have to ready your children. Help them get into work clothes (clothes you won't mind getting dirty), tie their long hair back, and hand everyone aprons.

5. Teach Your Kids About Food Hygiene: Endeavor that your kids wash their hands before beginning any task, while touching food materials, such as raw, cooked, or ready-to-eat items, and after cooking.

6. No Hurries: Except for older and more experienced kids, don't expect things to be done quickly. As a matter of fact, prepare to be done later than usual. Plan more time and keep in mind that although long, the journey and destination are just as fun, especially with younger kids.

7. Expect it to Be Messy: Cooking isn't clean business, so don't expect having your kids in the kitchen is going to change that one bit. Even more than ever now, expect that the mess would be greater. But don't be discouraged because you have kids involved. You can prepare for damage control by using trays and plastic tablecloth to cover up the areas beneath their workstations. If you don't mind, you could also have more fun if you allow the mess to take its course and clean up the kitchen only cooking is done.

8. Make the Process Enjoyable: You're not Grumpy, so don't go all Hell's Kitchen on your kids. Allow a loving and relaxing environment where everyone is free to have fun and make mistakes. Kids are more likely to enjoy cooking when you're relaxed and prepared to have fun with them. If you feel uncomfortable or nervous with a meal, try a simpler one—it's still learning for them either way. Also, don't be obtrusive. Step in only when it's of utmost necessity, otherwise allow them to enjoy the moment as they wish.

9. Engage Them in Conversations: A quiet kitchen doesn't help anyone. It only creates tension and ruins the purpose of spending time together. You can indulge your older kids by having them read our recipes and steps beforehand, and fetch the ingredients and tools needed. Talk through the process and make plans for each child to manage different tasks. Additionally, you can explain the dish you're making and show them pictures to give them an inkling of what can be expected at the end of the day. This will create, in the child, a sense of purpose and understanding.

The Age Grade Guide to Cooking With Kids

The ability of children to participate varies across different cooking tasks. Using your sense of judgment, assign children to tasks befitting their capacity, size, age, and experience. You want them to be safe at all times, so it's imperative that you ensure that the activities they undertake don't put them at risk.

1. Under Three-Year-Olds: Children under the age of three may not be ready to go to the toilet on their own or pick and wear clothes, but they're some of the most when it comes to helping out in the kitchen. You can take advantage of this inclination to impart some kitchen culture and have some fun. Once you get them settled into the process and continue with your normal things, you'll have a great time cooking with them. To ensure things go swimmingly, clear out any potential hazards nearby. Keep hot liquids and foods, cleaning products, pot handles, and heavy or sharp tools away from their grabbing hands.

Think about what they could trip over or reach easily. Also, ensure that the path is always clear whenever you're moving with something heavy, sharp, or hot. Feel free to put them on the kitchen table so they can be safely away from hazards. With the way clear, feel free to teach them about food, kitchen culture, and etiquette, and help them get familiar with the environment.

Below are some activities to indulge children in this category with:

- Using a potato masher to mash foods. Take note to not give them overly hot items.

- Spoon ingredients for scaling. You'd be surprised how fun the process can be; you can also sneak in some math lessons here.

- Wash plastic items and vegetables. You can teach your kids the names of vegetables and other items around the kitchen this way. This could improve their inclination to try new foods and encourage them to adopt healthy kitchen culture.

- Stirring ingredients; only give them room-temperature ingredients to mix.

- Sprinkling food with icing sugar, cake decorations, and flour. Use a tray to catch any mess they make.

2. Three to Five-Year-Olds: Children in this category are more mature and have better common sense. Thus, they can follow instructions better and acquire more skills. Although skill sets vary greatly for kids this age, your knowledge of your child and their capacity is key. At this stage, many kids aren't nearly interested in what you have to say about anything. You may have impulsive toddlers on your hands, so take care to ensure they're always safe. Don't let them do activities you aren't sure they're capable of. Activities suitable for kids in this age bracket include:

- Washing vegetables and fruits

- Cutting soft items, such as strawberries, butter, and mushrooms with blunt or plastic knives.

- Weighing ingredients by pouring them into scales with measuring spoons.

- Mixing ingredients with their hands or other utensils. Don't make them mix extremely cold or hot ingredients.

- Tearing and squashing herbs, vegetables, and fruits.

- Sieving. Teach them to balance sieves over bowls and tap instead of shaking to drain.

- Kneading dough. Kids this age can handle some light kneading, but you'll have to do round up the task to ensure the dough is well kneaded.

- Using a mortar and pestle. Hand them the light, wooden ones rather than the heavier or breakable ones.

- Applying spread to bread or icing to cakes.

- Hulling and picking food items like leaves, strawberries, grapes, tomatoes, broad beans, and more.

3. Eight to Eleven-Year-Olds: At the age of eight and above, children can start to get more involved in the planning and carrying out of activities in the kitchen. They have a bit more independence and will require less supervision than kids younger than them. However, they aren't fully grown and still have to be supervised and protected from hazards. Ensure to employ a hands-off approach when needed.
Activities suitable for kids at these ages are:

- Using a peeler

- Using appliances like microwaves and ovens

- Opening cans

- Fetching ingredients from refrigerators, fridges, and cupboards

- Planning a family meal

- Reading out and following recipes

- Making some salads

- Whisking ingredients with a handheld nicer or balloon whisk

4. Twelve-Year-Olds and up: At the age of 12 and above, kids can be trusted to prepare more complex meals and even begin experimenting on their own. Their abilities at this stage are only limited to their imagination and how inclined they are to the art of cooking, as well as to their experience. Kids at this age don't require as much supervision as younger ones but shouldn't be allowed to sail free either. Minor supervision is needed to prevent any accidents.

Chapter 4: Breakfast Recipes

Whether you agree that breakfast trumps every other meal or not, eating right in the morning is unarguably a great way to kickstart your day. That focus, inspiration, and energy you need to be productive can all be improved or damaged by the kind, quality, and quantity of food you have in the morning. This is because blood sugar, which is mostly responsible for our needed energy boost, is usually at its lowest in the morning; quite expectedly so too, since you've not had anything to eat in more than 10 hours—if you eat dinner and go to bed early, of course.

If you are also concerned about your weight, then you want to take breakfast seriously. What you eat in the morning will not magically make you thinner, but it ensures that you are able to control all that you will eat for the rest of the day. For instance, eating something filling in the morning will grant you better control over your appetite during lunch and dinner.

Knowing the importance of a healthy breakfast, you might think it wise to train your kids to also appreciate eating right in the morning. For proper physical and mental development, children need to feed on as many nutrients as possible. This is why you, as the parent, need to be intentional about breakfast. This means a balanced diet, like the ones that are shared below.

These DASH breakfast recipes are just what you need to get your mind and body ready for a successful day. Give them a go!

Parisian Ham and Cheese Egg Cups

Prep 30 min | cook 20 min

Ingredients

100g golden caster sugar

1 tbsp plain flour

zest and juice 2 oranges

- ½ tsp pepper
- ¼ tsp ground nutmeg
- 1 ¼ cups chopped croissant
- 3 oz diced deli ham
- 3 oz grated cheese, preferably Gruyere
- 2 large eggs
- Cooking spray

Method

1. Ensure that your oven is preheated to 350°F.

2. Using cooking spray, lightly grease a 12-cup muffin pan.

3. Fill each muffin cup—it shouldn't reach the top—with ham, cheese, and croissant.

4. Crack eggs open into a small bowl and sprinkle with nutmeg. Sprinkle some pepper and whisk.

5. Next, add the egg mixture to each muffin cup and place the pan in the preheated oven for 20 minutes.

6. This breakfast can be served immediately. It can also be sealed in an airtight container and preserved for up to three days in a refrigerator.

Nutritional Information

Each muffin cup contains:

92 cal | 7g protein | 3g carbs | 0g fiber | 6g fat | 3g sat. fat | 416.5mg sodium

Quiche Lorraine With Hash Brown Crust

Prep 30 min | cook 1 hr 12 min

Ingredients

- ¼ cup fresh flat-leaf parsley, chopped
- 1 lb frozen hash browns, thawd and torn
- ¾ cup Swiss cheese, shredded
- 4 tbsp melted unsalted butter
- 1 pinch cayenne pepper
- Kosher salt
- 1 pinch nutmeg
- Ground black pepper
- ½ cup heavy cream
- 6 slices bacon, minced in ¼ inch pieces
- ½ cup sour cream
- 1 tbsp extra virgin olive oil
- 3 large eggs
- 1 diced onion

Method

1. Ensure that the oven is preheated to 400°F.

2. Using a clean kitchen towel, squeeze out moisture from the shredded hash browns.

3. Add the hash browns, ¼ tsp of salt and pepper, and melted butter into a 9-inch pie plate. Mix well to combine. Press down on this mixture and flatten on the sides of the pie plate.

4. Place in the oven to bake for about 35 minutes. After this period, reduce the oven heat to 350°F.

5. Set your stove to medium-high heat and place the skillet containing the bacon pieces on it. Allow to cook for 5 minutes. Then, line a plate with a paper towel and place the cooked bacon on it to cool down.

6. Clean out the skillet, reduce the heat to medium, and add the olive oil. Stir onions into the hot oil and cook covered for 6 minutes. Watch the onions and stir occasionally. Open the skillet and stir for an additional 6 minutes, or until the sides

7. Add nutmeg, cayenne, heavy cream, eggs, pepper, salt, and sour cream into a large bowl and whisk. Next add parsley, bacon, cheese, and onion, and stir well.

8. With a spoon, take from this cream mixture and spread over the baked hash brown. Let it bake for 20 minutes.

9. Remove the pan from the oven and set it aside for 10 minutes. Serve.

Nutritional Information

Each serving contains:

384 cal | 12g protein | 16g carbs | 2g fiber | 30.5g fat | 16g sat. fat | 470mg sodium

DASH KIDS LUNCH BREAK

Sunny-Side Up Pizza

Prep 10 min | cook 17 min

Ingredients	Method
•4 large eggs	1. Make sure the oven is preheated to 450°F.
•Cornmeal	2. Prepare a baking sheet by dusting it with cornmeal.
•1 bunch spinach, stems removed	3. Flour a clean surface and place pizza dough on it. Mold into a circle, then place on the pan.
•Flour	
•4 oz deli ham, minced	4. Add mustard to the dough and top by sprinkling ¾ cup of Gruyere cheese. Add ham and spinach, and sprinkle the remaining cheese.
•1 lb pizza dough	
•4 oz Gruyere cheese, shredded	5. One at a time, break eggs into a bowl and place on the pizza without whisking.
•1 tbsp Dijon mustard	6. Bake for about 17 minutes, by which time the egg whites should have set sunny-side up. Serve.
	Nutritional Information
	Each serving contains:
	508 cal	31g protein	55g carbs	3g fiber	17.5g fat	7g sat. fat	1056m sodium

Granola Bars

Prep 10 min | cook 20min

Ingredients

- ½ cup dark chocolate chips
- 2 cups whole rolled oats
- ½ cup dried cherries
- 1 ½ tsp pure vanilla extract
- 1 cup diced almonds
- 1 cup raisins
- ¼ cup honey
- ½ cup almond butter

Method

1. Preheat the oven to 350°F.

2. Prepare a baking pan by lining it with parchment paper.

3. Place the rolled oats on a baking sheet and spread them. Let it bake in the oven for about 10 minutes, then set it aside to cool for a bit. Afterward, transfer the baked oats to a bowl.

4. Steep your raisins in hot water for about 10 minutes before draining them. Put the raisins in your food processor until it becomes a smooth puree. Add the vanilla, almond butter, honey, and pulse until well mixed.

5. Turn this mixture into the bowl containing baked oats. Add almonds, chocolate chips, and dried cherries and combine until you get a dense mixture. Spread this mixture onto your lined baking pan and leave it in your oven for about an hour.

6. Take out of the pan and you should be able to divide them into 14 granola bars. They can be stored in an airtight container and at room temperature for about one week.

Nutritional Information

Each bar contains:

273 cal | 6g protein | 35g carbs | 5g fiber | 14g fat | 3g sat. fat | 150mg sodium

Salmon and Dill Egg Cups

Prep 20 min | cook 20 min

Ingredients

- ½ tsp pepper
- 3 farmer's cheese (or 2 oz cold Neufchatel cheese), cut into small pieces
- 3 oz smoked salmon, minced
- ¼ cup fresh dill, diced
- Egg base
- Cooking spray

Method

1. Make sure your oven is preheated to 350°F.

2. Prepare your 12-cup muffin pan by oiling it with cooking spray.

3. Into each cup of your muffin pan, add the cheese, dill, salmon, and egg base. Finally, top with some sprinkle of pepper.

4. Pop the muffin pan in the oven and leave for about 20 minutes. Your salmon and dill eggs should swell and be slightly golden.

5. You can serve immediately and enjoy while hot. This meal can also be sealed in an airtight container and refrigerated for 3 days.

Nutritional Information

Each muffin cup contains:

52 cal | 5g protein | 1g carbs | 0g fiber | 4g fat | 2g sat. fat | 147mg sodium

Quiche Biscuits With Bacon, Cheddar, and Chives

Prep 10 min | cook 40 min

Ingredients

- 2 tbsp fresh chives, chopped
- 4 cups cauliflower florets
- 4 strips cooked turkey bacon, crumbled
- ½ cup almond flour, blanched
- 2 tbsp unsalted butter
- 1 tsp baking powder
- 2 beaten egg whites
- ½ tsp kosher salt
- ½ cup 2%, reduced-fat sharp cheddar cheese, grated
- Nonstick cooking spray

Method

1. Make sure your oven is preheated to 400°F, and prepare a 6-cup muffin pan by lightly oiling it with cooking spray.

2. Put your cauliflower florets in a medium-sized bowl and add 2 tbsp of water. Microwave for about 10 minutes, by which time the cauliflower should be much softer.

3. Drain all the water from the bowl and, using a fork, beat the cauliflower until smooth and mushy. Set it aside to cool for a bit, before squeezing out moisture from the cauliflower with a clean kitchen towel.

4. Add salt, almond flour, and baking powder to the cauliflower and combine. Stir in melted butter, shredded cheese, and egg whites into the mixture in the bowl, before incorporating chives and bacon.

5. With clean hands, mold cheese mixture into six round doughs. Place them on your muffin pan, and lightly press down on the balls to flatten them.

6. Bake for 25 minutes or until the top turns light brown. Let it sit for 5 minutes before placing it on a cooling rack.

7. The biscuits can be wrapped and preserved in a freezer for two months. Microwave when ready to eat.

Nutritional Information

Each quiche biscuit contains

150 cal | 8g protein | 6g carbs | 2g fiber | 11g fat | 4g sat. fat | 320mg sodium

Yogurt Parfaits

Prep 5 min | cook 2h 6 min

Ingredients

- ¼ cup toasted almonds
- 1 cup pomegranate juice
- ½ cup pomegranate seeds
- 1/3 cups chia seeds
- 6 oz raspberries
- 2 tbsp honey
- 6 oz blueberries
- 4 cups nonfat plain Greek yogurt

Method

1. Add pomegranate juice, honey, and chia seeds into a saucepan and mix well to combine.

2. Set stove to medium-high heat, and place your saucepan on it. When it begins to boil, reduce the medium-low. Stir for 3 minutes.

3. Turn off the stove and pour the content of your saucepan into an airtight container. Put this container into a refrigerator for 2 hours, or until it sets into a jam consistency.

4. You can get 4 serving cups and, in this order, add your Greek yogurt, jam, both berries, pomegranate seeds, and almonds.

5. Best enjoyed if refrigerated for 3 days before serving.

Nutritional Information

Each serving cup contains:

347 cal | 31g protein | 50g carbs | 7g fiber | 8g fat | 1g sat. fat | 130mg sodium

Ham and Cheese Scones

Prep 13 min | cook 22 min

Ingredients

- 1 cup cold heavy cream (extra 1 tbsp for coating)
- 2 cup all-purpose flour
- 1 tbsp fresh thyme (a little extra for sprinkling)
- 1 tbsp baking powder
- 3 oz minced ham
- 2 tsp sugar
- 3 oz sharp cheddar cheese, shredded
- ½ tsp kosher salt
- 4 tbsp cold unsalted butter, diced
- ½ tsp black pepper (extra for sprinkling)

Method

1. Make sure your oven is preheated to 400°F. Also, prepare a baking sheet by lining it with parchment paper.

2. Add baking powder, salt, pepper, sugar, and flour into a large bowl and whisk.

3. Using your fingers, mix the unsalted butter into the flour until crumbs are formed. Add thyme, ham, heavy cream, and cheese and stir until well combined. If done well, the crumbs should disappear to form a smooth dough.

4. Flatten the dough on a clean surface and divide into eight triangles. Place each triangle onto the baking sheet. Coat the top of the dough with the remaining heavy cream. Sprinkle with extra black pepper and thyme.

5. Bake in the preheated oven for about 22 minutes.

Nutritional Information

Each scone contains:

335 cal | 8g protein | 28g carbs | 1g fiber | 21.5g fat | 13.5g sat fat | 520mg sodium
Ham and Cheese Scones

Egg Pepper Rings With Carrot Sa[lsa]

Prep 7 min | cook 13 min

Ingredients

- ½ tsp dried oregano
- 2 medium red bell peppers
- 8 large peppers
- 2 tbsp extra virgin olive oil
- ½ cup fresh cilantro, torn
- 2 large carrots, shredded
- Kosher salt
- 16 oz grape tomatoes, cut into 4 parts
- 1 garlic clove, diced
- Pepper

Method

1. Cut 8 rings out of your bell peppers; they should be ½ inch thick. Dice what is left of the peppers and put everything in a medium-sized bowl.

2. Set your stove to medium heat and place a nonstick skillet on it. Heat 1 tbsp of olive oil in the pan. Cook both sides of the pepper rings in the hot oil for 4 minutes or until they are tender.

3. Add the diced peppers, carrots, garlic, tomatoes, a pinch of salt and pepper, and the remaining oil into a medium bowl. Add cilantro and fold in well.

4. Break an egg into the holes of the pepper rings, and sprinkle with a pinch of salt and pepper. Also, top with oregano. Cover the skillet and cook for 5 minutes.

5. Top with the salsa in the bowl and serve. You can enjoy it with English muffins.

Nutritional Information

Each serving contains:

250 cal | 14g protein | 11g carbs | 3g fiber | 16.5g fa]t | 4g sat. fat | 320mg sodium

Salsa and Sausage Egg Cups

Prep 20 min | cook 20 min

Ingredients

- ½ tsp pepper
- 6 z frozen hash browns, torn
- ¼ cup fresh salsa
- 3 oz dried chorizo, chopped
- Egg base
- Cooking spray

Method

1. Make sure your oven is preheated to 350°F.

2. Oil a 12-cup muffin pan with your cooking spray and add chorizo egg base, and hash browns to each cup. Top with salsa and a sprinkle of pepper.

3. Put the pan in the preheated oven for about 20 minutes. During this time, your sausage eggs should have achieved a golden-brown color. They should also be puffed.

4. You can serve immediately. Also, place in an airtight container and preserve in a refrigerator for 3 days.

Nutritional Information

Each muffin cup contains:

82 cal | 4g protein | 5g carbs | 1g fiber | 6g fat | 2g sat. fat | 226mg sodium

Baked and Spiced Oatmeal

Prep 10 min | cook 30 min

Ingredients

- 2 pears, divided into ½ inch wedges
- 2 cups whole rolled oats
- ½ tsp kosher salt
- 2 cups plain unsweetened almond milk
- ¾ tsp cardamom
- ¼ cup maple syrup
- 1 tsp baking powder
- 1 ¼ tsp pumpkin pie spice
- 1 tsp pure vanilla extract
- Cooking spray

Method

1. Make sure your oven is preheated to 375°F. Also, prepare a standard baking pan by coating it with the oil spray.]

2. Mix cardamom, salt, almond milk, syrup, oats, pumpkin pie spice, baking powder, and vanilla in a large bowl. When well combined, transfer the mixture to your baking pan. Top with the pear wedges.

3. Next, bake in your preheated oven until the oats mixture swells a little and is tender. This should last for about 30 minutes.

4. Top with a drizzle of maple syrup and enjoy. If kept in an airtight container, your baked oatmeal can be refrigerated for 4 days.

Nutritional Information

Each serving contains:

222 cal | 5g protein | 41g carbs | 6g fiber | 5g fat | 1g sat. fat | 203mg sodium

DASH KIDS LUNCH BREAK

Banana Cream Pie Overnight Oats

Prep 5 min | cook 6 min

Ingredients

- 1 tsp pure vanilla extract
- 1 peeled ripe banana, diced
- 1 tbsp chia seeds
- ½ cup low-fat whipped cottage cheese
- ¼ cup old-fashioned oats
- ¼ cup unsweetened soy milk
- Unsweetened coconut, shredded

Method

1. Microwave your banana in a small bowl for 30 seconds. By this time, it should be considerably tender.

2. Add the cheese to the banana and mash until it forms a well-combined paste.

3. Mix vanilla, oats milk, and chia seeds into the paste, cover the bowl, and leave in your refrigerator for 6 hours (you can make ahead and leave overnight).

4. Top with shredded coconut and serve.

Nutritional Information

Each serving contains:

340 cal | 21g protein | 46g carbs | 10g fiber | 9g fat | 1.5g sat. fat | 550mg sodium

Apple-Raisin French Toast

Prep 30 min | cook 20 min

Ingredients	Method
• 4 large eggs • 1 large sandwich roll, chopped to fill 1 ¼ cup • ½ tsp ground cinnamon • ½ apple, chopped to fill ¾ cup • 3 tbsp sugar • 3 tbsp raisins • ¼ cup heavy cream • Cooking spray	1. Make sure your oven is preheated to 350°F. 2. Oil a 12-cup muffin pan with a cooking spray, and add raisins, sandwich roll, and chopped apples into each cup. 3. Make your egg base and mix cinnamon, sugar, and heavy cream into it. Add this mixture to the muffin cups and bake. 4. After 20 minutes, your French toast should be puffed and brown. 5. You can enjoy it while it's hot or set it aside to cool for a bit. It can be preserved for 3 days if sealed in an airtight container and refrigerated. Nutritional Information Each cup contains: 78 cal | 3g protein | 9g carbs | 1g fiber | 4g fat | 2g sat. fat | 218mg sodium

Gluten-Free Stewed Peppers and Toma-toes With Eggs

Prep 20 min | cook 31 min

Ingredients

- 4 corn tortillas
- 2 tbsp extra virgin olive oil
- 8 large eggs
- 1 medium onion, diced
- 28 oz can whole tomatoes
- 1 red bell pepper, chopped into small squares
- 4 garlic cloves, minced
- 1 orange bell pepper, chopped into small squares
- Black pepper
- Kosher salt

Method

1. Set stove to medium heat and place a large skillet on it. Pour olive oil into the pan and, after it has heated up a bit, add the onion. Cover the skillet and cook for 4 minutes.

2. Add red and orange peppers into the pan with ½ tsp of salt and pepper each. Cover again and cook for 8 minutes, then stir in garlic and cook open for a minute.

3. Press the tomatoes in the pan and leave to boil. Reduce the heat to medium-low and allow to simmer for 5 minutes.

4. Using a spoon, make 8 holes in the sauce. Break the eggs into each hole, cover the pan, and simmer for 6 minutes. Then cook open for an additional 7 minutes, or until the eggs are done.

5. Cover the tortillas with slightly moist paper towels, and leave them in the microwave for about 20 seconds.

6. Serve stewed peppers with corn tortillas.

Nutritional Information

Each serving contains:

351 cal | 18g protein | 29g carbs | 4g fiber | 17g fat | 4g sat. fat | 808mg sodium

Ham Casserole

Prep 15 min | cook 1 hr 55 min

Ingredients

- 2 ½ cups whole milk
- 8 oz sliced whole wheat Italian bread
- ¼ tsp cayenne
- 6 oz minced Canadian bacon
- ¼ tsp ground nutmeg
- 2 cups Swiss chard leaves, shredded
- 4 tsp Dijon mustard
- 4 oz shredded Gouda cheese
- 10 large eggs
- 1 cup grape tomatoes
- Cooking spray

Method

1. Preheat your oven to 350°F.

2. Prepare a 9 by 13-inch baking pan with cooking spray.

3. Cover the pan with sliced Italian bread, then add ham, Swiss chard, and Gouda cheese to each slice. Finally, top with tomatoes.

4. Add the eggs, pepper, salt, cayenne, nutmeg, and mustard into a medium-sized bowl and whisk. Add milk and whisk again.

5. Pour the mixture in the bowl over the bread in the pan. Let it sit for an hour.

6. Afterward, bake until it swells and achieves a golden brown color. This should take 40 minutes.

7. Remove from the oven and let it stand for about 15 minutes. Serve.

8. You can divide the casserole into small squares and store it in an airtight container. It can be refrigerated for up to 4 days.

Nutritional Information

Each serving contains:

296 cal | 20g protein | 20g carbs | 2g fiber | 15g fat | 7g sat. fat | 1036mg sodium

Tater Tot Pizza

Prep 10 min | cook 27 min

Ingredients

- Cornmeal
- 1 lb pizza dough
- Flour
- 1 cup frozen potato tots
- 6 large eggs
- 1 ½ tbsp extra virgin olive oil
- 4 oz Gruyere cheese, roughly shredded
- 1 small onion, diced
- 4 oz deli ham, minced
- 1 small red pepper plus 1 small green pepper, diced
- 1 jalapeno pepper, cut into rings
- Kosher salt
- Pepper

Method

1. Preheat the oven to 425°F.

2. Add 1 tsp of oil to a baking sheet and add potato tots. Toss it to coat the potatoes. Place in the oven to roast for about 10 minutes. Halfway, turn the potatoes.

3. Increase the oven to 450°F.

4. Add ¼ tsp of both salt and pepper. Also, put in peppers, onions, oil, jalapeno, and cheese. Mix well to combine.

5. Prepare a baking sheet by dusting it with cornmeal.

6. Dust a clean surface with flour and place pizza dough on it. Shape dough into an oval that is 16 inches thick. Place on the baking sheet and top with the mixture in your bowl. Also, add potato tots and ham. Sprinkle remaining Gruyere cheese.

7. Crack one egg into each jalapeno ring. Bake for about 17 minutes, or until the eggs set. Serve hot.

Nutritional Information

Each serving contains:

430 cal | 20g protein | 41g carbs | 3g fiber | 19g fat | 6g sat. fat | 1140 sodium

Peanut Butter and Jelly Bars

Prep 10 min | cook 30 min

Ingredients	Method
• 1/3 cup strawberry jam	1. Make sure your oven is preheated to 350°F.
• 15 oz can low-sodium chickpeas	2. Prepare a baking pan by lining it with parchment paper. Allow some overhang on opposite sides of the pan.
• ½ tsp kosher salt	3. Add honey, vanilla, peanut butter, and chickpeas to a food processor, and pulse until you get a smooth consistency.
• 2 tbsp honey	
• ¼ tsp baking soda	4. Combine baking soda, peanuts, baking powder, peanuts, oats, and salt in a small bowl. When well mixed, transfer to the food processor and mix some more.
• 2 tsp pure vanilla extract	
• 1 tsp baking powder	5. Separate 1 cup of the baking soda mixture into a bowl as your reserve. From the dough still in the food processor, press some onto your pan.
• ½ cup peanut butter	
• ½ cup unsalted peanuts, roasted	6. Lather jam on the dough and scatter your reserve dough on the jam. Bake for about 30 minutes, or until it achieves a light brown color and the top is set.
• 2/3 cup old-fashioned rolled oats	
	7. Let it sit for 15 minutes before transferring to a cooling rack. Only slice after PB&J is completely cool. Divide into 16 bars before serving.
	8. These PB&J bars should be stored in airtight containers. They can be preserved for 3 days at room temperature or 5 days in a refrigerator.
	Nutritional Information
	Each bar contains:
	140 cal	5g protein	16g carbs	2g fiber	7g fat	1g sat. fat	0mg sodium

Pimiento, Cheese, and Ham Scramble

Prep 15 min | cook 7 min

Ingredients

- 2 tbsp cream cheese
- 8 large eggs
- 2 oz extra sharp cheddar cheese
- 1 tsp hot sauce
- 2 scallions
- Kosher salt
- 1 medium red pepper, roasted
- Pepper
- 3 oz deli ham, minced
- 1 tbsp unsalted butter, melted

Method

1. Crack eggs into a large bowl and whisk in hot sauce, salt, pepper, and 1 tbsp water.

2. Set your stove to medium heat and place a nonstick skillet containing oil on it.

3. Place ham in the pan and cook for about 3 minutes. Stir and toss occasionally. Add the red pepper and cook for an additional minute. Transfer the ingredients in the skillet to a plate.

4. Transfer the mixture in the large bowl to the pan and stir for about 3 minutes. Add both cheese, scallions, and the ingredients in the plate, and fold.

Nutritional Information

Each serving contains:

305 cal | 20g proteins | 4g carbs | 1g fiber | 22.5g fat | 8.5g sat. fat | 810mg sodium

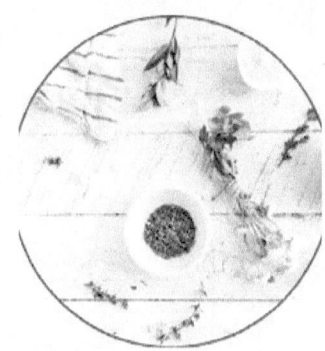

Cheese and Herb Quiche

Prep 10 min | cook 2HR 15 min

Ingredients	Method
• ½ cup flat-leaf parsley, diced	To make the pie crust:
• 2 ¼ cup all-purpose flour	1. Make sure your oven is preheated to 375°F.
• 2 tbsp chopped chives	2. Add flour, butter, and salt into a food processor. Mix until it forms crumbs.
• 4 ½ oz extra-sharp cheddar cheese, shredded	3. Pour ice water into the processor and mix until the crumbs combine into one whole dough.
• ¾ cups frozen unsalted butter, thawed and cubed	4. Slice the dough in half and mold each into rectangles. They should be at least ½ inch thick. Wrap and cool them in your refrigerator for 30 minutes.
• 2 cup whole milk	5. Take the dough out of the refrigerator and, after flouring a clean surface, roll them to be, at least, 16 by
• 2 tbsp olive oil	
• 1 cup crème fraîche	7-inch thick rectangles. Place them in tart pans that have removable bottoms and cut off excess dough. Keep in your refrigerator for another 20 minutes.
• ¼ cup ice water	
• 1 medium onion, minced	6. Put the tart pans on a large baking sheet, cover with aluminum foil, and place pie weights on them. After baking for about 15 minutes, remove both aluminum foil and pie weights. Bake for an additional 10 minutes or until they turn light brown.
• 4 large eggs	
• Kosher salt	
• ½ tsp kosher salt (for the filling)	
• Pepper	7. Take the baking sheet out and allow to cool on a wire rack. Turn down the temperature of the oven to 325°F.

To make the filling:

1. Set stove to medium heat and balance a large skillet containing olive oil on it.

2. Add onion and a pinch of both salt and pepper to the pan. Cover the skillet and allow it to cook for 10 minutes. Stir occasionally.

3. Open the pan and caramelize for an additional 10 minutes. Take down the skillet and set it aside to cool.

4. Crack eggs into a bowl and add crème fraîche, pepper, milk, and ¼ tsp of salt. Whisk well before adding in cheese, parsley, and chives. Stir well to combine.

5. Pour this mixture into the tart shells and allow to bake for 40 minutes.

6. Take it out of the oven and let it sit for about 10 minutes, then serve. Keep in an airtight container and refrigerate for up to 3 months.

Nutritional Information

Each serving contains:

275 cal | 6g protein | 16g carbs | 1g fiber | 20.5g fat | 11.5g sat. fat | 180mg sodium

Lemon Poppy Seed Jelly Doughnuts

Prep 35 min | cook 1HR 15 min

Ingredients	Method
• 1 cup strawberry jam • ¾ cup whole milk • 2 tsp lemon zest • 2 ¼ tsp active dry yeast • 3 tbsp poppy seeds • 1 ¼ cup sugar • 64 oz canola oil (extra for coating) • 2 large eggs • 3 ½ cups all-purpose flour • 2 tbsp unsalted butter, diced and softened • 1 tsp kosher salt	1. In a small microwave-safe bowl, add milk and heat to about 110°F. Stir in ¼ cup of sugar and yeast and allow to sit for 5 minutes. 2. Get an electric mixer and add already beaten eggs, butter, and salt to the mixer bowl. Combine. 3. Put ½ flour, 1 tsp lemon zest, and 1 tbsp poppy seeds into the bowl and stir until dough forms. Pour in the remaining flour while stirring. 4. Reduce setting of the electric stand mixer to the lowest and, with a dough hook, stir for about 5 minutes. The dough should be considerably sticky. 5. Coat a large bowl with canola oil and add the dough. Using a damp towel, cover the bowl and leave it through the night in your refrigerator. It should double in size. You can also leave it at room temperature for 1 hour. 6. Lightly grease a baking sheet and set aside. 7. Flour a clean surface and roll dough on it until about ½ inch thick. Using a 3-inch cutter, slice out circles and place them on the oiled sheet. Roll what is left of the dough and repeat this process. 8. Cover the baking sheet with a slightly moist clean towel,

and leave to rise at room temperature for 30 minutes.

9. Set stove to medium heat. Add oil to a large saucepan and place it on the stove to get hot.

10. Place 2 tbsp poppy seeds, 2 tsp lemon zest, and 1 cup sugar in a large bowl and whisk vigorously.

11. Place doughnuts in the saucepan and cook each side for about a minute. When they're done, transfer the bowl of zest mixture and toss to coat. Then place on a baking sheet to cool.

12. Get a piping bag that has a ½ inch tip and fill it with strawberry jam. Cut tiny holes in each doughnut and squeeze jam into each.

Nutritional Information

Each doughnut contains:

485 cal | 8g protein | 81g carbs | 2g fiber | 15g fat | 3.5g sat. fat | 270mg sodium

Raspberry Smoothie Bowls

Prep 5 min | cook 0 min

Ingredients

- Toasted coconut flakes
- 2 cup frozen raspberries
- ½ cup low-fat milk
- 2 bananas
- 1 tbsp chia seeds
- ½ cup nonfat Greek yogurt

Method

1. Add yogurt, raspberries, bananas, milk, and chia seeds into a blender. Puree until you get a smooth mixture.

2. The smoothie should fill 2 bowls. Top with coconut flakes.

Nutritional Information

Each smoothie bowl contains:

209 cal | 9g protein | 4g carbs | 8g fiber | 1g fat | 0.5g sat. fat | 49mg sodium

Buttermilk Waffle, Bacon, and Egg Sandwich

Prep 10 min | cook 15 min

Ingredients

- Maple syrup
- ¾ cup all-purpose flour
- 2 cup baby spinach
- 1 ½ tsp baking powder
- 16 slices cooked bacon
- 1 tsp baking soda
- 4 tbsp melted unsalted butter
- ¼ tsp kosher salt
- 1 ¾ cup buttermilk
- 10 large eggs

Method

1. Make sure your oven is preheated to 200°F.

2. Add flour, baking soda, baking powder, and salt into a medium-sized bowl. Mix well.

3. Crack 2 eggs into a large bowl. Keeping the yolks for later, whisk the egg whites in an electric mixer for about 2 minutes, or until it forms a peak.

4. Add buttermilk and unsalted butter to the yolks in the bowl. Also, add the flour and mix vigorously. Pour in the egg whites and gently fold.

5. Using a waffle maker and following the instructions on the manual, cook until the waffles turn light brown.

6. Line a baking sheet with aluminum foil and place the waffles in the pan. Warm in your preheated oven.

7. Cook the remaining eggs sunny-side up. Make into sandwiches, starting with waffles, eggs, bacon, and spinach. You can top with a drizzle of maple syrup.

Nutritional Information

Each sandwich contains:

316 cal | 17g protein | 13g carbs | 0g fiber | 21g fat | 9g sat. fat| 751mg sodium

Sugared Waffles With Sautéed Maple Apples

Ingredients

- ½ cup toasted pecans
- 2 tbsp unsalted butter
- Pinch ground cinnamon
- 2 Gala apples, dice
- 1 tbsp brown sugar
- ¼ cup maple syrup

For the waffles:

- ¼ cup unsalted butter, melted
- ¼ tsp ground cinnamon
- 4 frozen and thawed dinner rolls
- ¼ cup granulated sugar
- Nonstick cooking spray

Method

1. Set your stove to medium heat and place a large skillet on it. Melt the unsalted butter in the pan, then add the apples and cook for about 4 minutes. By this time, they would have turned light brown.

2. Add 2 tbsp of water to the pan and cook until it dries up.

3. Add cinnamon, maple syrup, and brown sugar to the skillet and cook until the apples are soft. This should take 4 minutes.

4. Turn off the stove and set the pan down. Break pecans and add to the pan. Fold

To make the waffles:

1. Preheat the waffles maker to medium.

2. Add sugar and cinnamon into a small bowl, and mix.

3. Coat each dinner roll in butter, let the excess oil drip off, and toss in the cinnamon mixture.

4. Oil waffle iron with cooking spray, then add rolls. Allow to cook for about 2 minutes or until they turn slightly golden.

5. Place the waffles on clean plates and top with maple apples. Serve with whipped cream.

Nutritional Information

Each serving contains:

505 cal | 5g protein | 6g carbs | 4g fiber | 24g fat | 9.5g sat. fat | 226mg sodium

Eggs and Tater Bake

Prep 25 min | cook 50 min

Ingredients	Method
• 2 oz extra sharp cheddar cheese, shredded	1. Preheat your oven to 400°F.
• 4 cups frozen potato tots	2. Place potato tots on a rimmed baking sheet and leave them in the oven for 20 minutes.
• 8 large eggs	3. Set your stove to medium heat and place an oven-proof skillet over it. Heat oil in the pan, then add onion and ½ tsp of both pepper and salt. Cover the pan and cook for about 5 minutes.
• 2 tbsp extra virgin olive oil	
• ½ bunch spinach, diced	
• 1 medium onion, chopped	
• 3 plum tomatoes, chopped into 1-inch pieces	4. Stir mushrooms and red pepper into the pan and cook until the veggies are soft. This should take up to 6 minutes.
• 1 red bell pepper, chopped into ¼ inch pieces	5. Add tomatoes and garlic, and continue cooking for another 1 minute. Add potato tots and spinach, and fold in well.
• 1 garlic clove, diced	6. With a spoon, create eight small gaps in the mixture and break eggs into these holes. Sprinkle cheddar cheese and bake for another 18 minutes. The egg yolks should be slightly runny.
• 8 oz white mushrooms, halved	
• Kosher salt	Nutritional Information
• Black pepper	Each serving contains:
	344 cal	14g protein	24g carbs	3g fiber	21g fat	6g sat. fat	701mg sodium

French Toast Bowls

Prep 15 min | cook 55 min

Ingredients	Method
• 6 oz pack small blueberries • 5 tbsp unsalted butter • 6 oz pack raspberries • 1 ½ cup whole milk • 12 slices white sandwich bread • 4 large eggs • ½ tsp kosher salt • 1/3 cup granulated sugar, plus 1 tbsp • 2 tsp pure vanilla extract	1. Make sure your oven is preheated to 350°F. 2. Prepare four 1 cup bowls that are safe for oven use by oiling them with 2 tbsp of butter. 3. Crack eggs into a large pitcher. Also, whisk in milk, vanilla, 1/3 cup of sugar, and salt. 4. Dust the crust from the bread slices and spread the remaining butter on one side of each one. Cut each slice diagonally to form two triangles. 5. Arrange about six bread triangles on the sides of your oven-safe bowl. Add the berries as toppings, then repeat for the other three bowls. 6. Drizzle the mixture in your pitcher on the bread. Sprinkle what is left of your sugar, and place bowls on a baking sheet. 7. Cover with foil and bake in your preheated oven for about 20 minutes. Remove foil and bake for an additional 35 minutes, or until the bread turns light brown and the custard sets. 8. Remove from the oven and serve. Nutritional Information Each bowl contains: 263 cal | 8g protein | 34g carbs | 3g fiber | 11g fat | 5.5g sat. fat | 355mg sodium

Boursin, Bacon, and Spinach Scrambled Eggs

Prep 10 min | cook 13 min

Ingredients

- 1 tbsp milk
- 2 slices bacon
- 2 large eggs
- ½ cup baby spinach
- 2 chives, diced
- 1 oz Boursin cheese

Method

1. Wrap bacon slices with two clean paper towels and place on a microwave-safe plate. Cook in your microwave for about 3 minutes, then take out the plate. Allow to cool, then scatter the bacon.

2. Into a 10-inch jar add spinach and half of both the cheese and chives. Keep in your refrigerator overnight.

3. Take the jar out of the refrigerator and add milk, eggs, and a pinch of both kosher salt and pepper into it. Screw the lid on and shake well to mix.

4. Open the jar and microwave for about 1 minute. If the ingredients in the jar have not set, place them in the microwave again for 15 seconds. Continue until it's ready.

5. Add bacon slices and what remains of your chives and cheese. Serve.

Nutritional Information

Each jar contains:

364 cal | 22g protein | 4g carbs | 1g fiber | 28g fat | 13.5g sat. fat | 764mg sodium

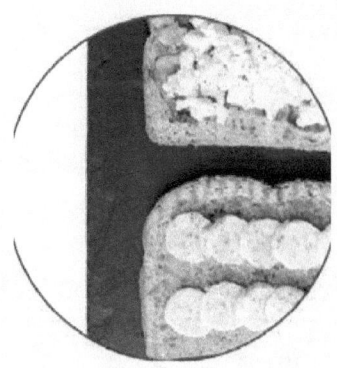

Mexican Scrambled Eggs

Prep 20 min | cook 3 min

Ingredients

- ½ small head romaine lettuce, leaves scattered
- 3 large tomatoes, diced
- 1 tbsp extra virgin olive oil
- ½ avocado, chopped into ½ inch bits
- 12 low salt tortilla chips, broken
- ½ small red onion, diced
- 8 large egg whites
- 4 egg yolks
- 1 small and seeded jalapeno, minced
- Black pepper
- ½ cup cilantro, cut roughly
- Kosher salt
- 2 tbsp fresh lime juice

Method

1. Pour lime juice into a medium bowl, and add cilantro, tomatoes, jalapeno, avocado, and onion. Also, mix in ¼ tsp of both salt and pepper.

2. Whisk egg whites, yolks, and 2 tbsp of water into a separate bowl. Stir in ½ tsp of pepper and ¼ tsp of salt. Add tortilla chips and mix.

3. Set your stove to medium heat and place a large skillet on it. Heat olive oil in the pan, then add the egg mixture. Stir until they are ready. This should take no more than 3 minutes, depending on your preference.

4. Add the salsa in the medium bowl on top of the eggs and serve with lettuce.

Nutritional Information

Each serving contains:

241 cal | 13 g protein | 18 carbs | 6g fiber | 14g fat | 3g sat. fat | 375mg sodium

Apple Spice Baked Oatmeal

Prep 10 min | cook 20 min

Ingredients

- 2 ½ cups old-fashioned rolled oats
- 1 ½ cups almond milk
- 1 ½ tsp ground nutmeg
- 1 cup applesauce
- 1 ½ tsp ground cinnamon
- 1 apple, finely chopped
- ¼ cup brown sugar
- ½ cup raisins
- 2 eggs
- ½ cup pecans
- ½ cup flaxseed meal

Method

1. Make sure your oven is preheated to 375°F. Also, prepare a 12-cup muffin pan by greasing it with olive oil.

2. Crack eggs into a small bowl and add brown sugar, milk, nutmeg, applesauce, cinnamon, raisins, flax meal, and pecans. Whisk thoroughly, then stir in oats. Set the bowl aside for 5 minutes and, using an ice cream scoop, add the mixture to the muffin cups.

3. Place the pan in your preheated oven and bake for about 20 minutes. Set the pan aside for 5 minutes before transferring to a cooling rack.

Nutritional Information

Each oatmeal cup contains:

196 cal | 5g protein | 28.2 carbs | 4.6 fiber | 8g fat | 1g sat. fat | 36.6mg sodium

Carrot Cake Oatmeal

Prep 15 min | cook 40 min

Ingredients

- ½ cup plain yogurt
- 4 cups water
- 1 tbsp brown sugar
- 1 cup steel-cut oats
- ¾ cup pecans, diced
- 1 apple, peeled, cored, and finely cut
- 1 tbsp butter
- ½ cup carrot, roughly chopped
- ⅛ tsp salt
- ½ cup raisins
- ½ tsp ground ginger
- 1 tsp ground cinnamon
- ½ tsp ground nutmeg

Method

1. Set your stove to medium-high and place a saucepan containing water on it.

2. When it starts to boil, stir in the steel-cut oats. Reduce heat to low and cook for 10 minutes. By this time, the oats should have risen and thickened a bit.

3. While the contents of the saucepan are cooking, set another stove to medium-low heat and place a skillet containing butter on it. Stir pecans.

4. Add cinnamon, chopped apples, ginger, carrot, salt, raisins, nutmeg, and salt into the pan. Allow this mixture to simmer on low heat for another 20 minutes.

5. While the contents of the saucepan are cooking, set another stove to medium-low heat and place a skillet containing butter on it. Cook the diced pecans in the hot oil for about 5 minutes or until the nuts turn light brown. Stir the pecans as they cook.

6. Add sugar to the pecans skillet and continue stirring until they melt completely.

7. Scoop oatmeal into six bowls and top each with 2 tbsp of the fried and sugared pecans. Also, add 1 tbsp of plain yogurt on top of each oatmeal.

Nutritional Information

Each bowl contains:

8.287 cal | 6.2g protein | 37.7 carbs | 13.9g fat | 2.7g sat. fat | 67.1mg sodium, and nutmeg into the pan, and continue to

Chapter 5: Lunch Recipes

Try as you might by making sure that your kids eat a healthy breakfast every morning, the fact is that there will most likely be some days when they (your children) miss that all too important morning meal. This might be as a result of a real emergency or simply because they woke up late and must hurry to school for a27 test. Such scenarios are quite common, and you shouldn't beat yourself up about it.

Regardless of the circumstance, the health and nutrition of your children remain a priority. This means that you must find a way to make up for their missing breakfast. However, this does not imply that you, as a parent, are only to take lunch seriously when your children did not eat breakfast. This afternoon meal, whether eaten at school or anywhere else, often makes up at least one-third of your kid's nutritional intake for the day (Schuna, n.d.). If lunch is neglected or compromised, this could adversely affect your child's growth and development.

The CDC, in a report on the connection between feeding habits and academic performance, revealed that a child's success at school can be greatly impacted by what they eat (Smith, 2020). While this isn't limited to lunch, the afternoon meal does contribute one-third of a child's overall daily nutrition. As such, you would agree that it's especially important.

While academic success and improved brain power are good things, providing a healthy lunch for your kids is also vital if they're athletically inclined. The more energy that's expended, the greater the need to replenish it for continued optimal performance. If, for instance, your kids don't have a well-made DASH lunch to rely on, they might look for unhealthy snacks. If your children are still at that impressionable age range, you want to influence them to always make healthy food choices; this begins by cooking lunch with them at home or packing them a healthy afternoon meal.

Hummus Avocado Wrap

Prep 5 min | cook 0 min

Ingredients

- 2 slices tomato
- 1 flour tortilla
- ¼ cup alfalfa sprouts
- 2 tbsp hummus
- ¼ avocado, minced
- Cucumber slices

Method

1. Place the flour tortilla on a small flat plate.

2. Spread hummus close to the center of the tortilla, then add tomato, avocado, alfalfa sprouts, and cucumber on top of the hummus.

3. Wrap tortilla and serve.

Note: If the flour tortilla is frozen, you can place it in a microwave for no more than 10 seconds or let it sit at room temperature for 2 hours. Also, as a result of the high calorie and sodium count in this meal, you can serve ½ Hummus Avocado Wrap to your child to stay within DASH guidelines.

Nutritional Information

Each wrap contains:

1300 cal | 27g protein | 170 carbs | 20g fiber | 31g fat | 8g sat. fat | 3200mg sodium

Cheddar Apple and Quesadillas

Prep 2 min | cook 5 min

Ingredients

- ½ cup cheddar cheese, grated
- 1 tbsp mayonnaise
- 1 small apple, minced
- 2 8-inch flour tortillas
- Nonstick cooking spray

Method

1. Lather both tortillas with mayonnaise and top one with apples and cheese. Cover with the remaining tortilla.

2. Set your stove to medium heat. Grease a skillet with cooking spray and place it on the stove.

3. Add quesadillas to the pan and cook for 3 minutes. By this time, the cheese should have melted. Turn the tortillas over and cook for another 2 minutes. The quesadillas should have a light brown color.

4. Turn the stove off, slice, and serve.

Nutritional Information

One quesadilla contains:

293 cal | 10g protein | 24g carbs | 1.8g fiber | 17.9g fat | 7.3g sat. fat | 489.1mg sodium

Beef Burritos

Prep 20 min | cook 9 min

Ingredients

- 8 whole-wheat burrito size tortillas
- 2 tsp extra virgin olive oil
- 1 cup cheddar cheese, grated
- 1 lb ground beef
- 16 oz refried beans
- 8 oz white mushrooms, diced
- ¾ cup homemade enchilada sauce
- 1 tbsp chili powder
- ½ tsp salt
- 1 tsp paprika
- ½ tsp onion powder
- 1 tsp cumin
- ½ tsp garlic powder

Method

olive oil and place on the pan.

2. Add beef and cook for 3 minutes or until it turns golden brown.

3. Put mushrooms, cumin, garlic powder, paprika, onion powder, salt, chili powder, and enchilada sauce into the pan and stir. Reduce heat to medium-low and cook for 5 minutes. Stir occasionally.

4. Add cheddar cheese and beans to the ingredients in the pan and cook while stirring for 1 minute.

5. Place tortillas on 8 small flat plates and add ½ cup of the mushroom mixture to each one. Let the mushroom mixture be a heap at the center of the tortillas. Top with cilantro, fold, and roll.

6. Burritos can be placed in a zip-top bag and stored in a freezer for 3 months.

Nutritional Information

Each burrito contains:

424 cal | 24g protein | 42g carbs | 7g fiber | 20g fat | 7g sat. fat | 927mg sodium

Asian Rice Salad

Prep 20 min | cook 2 min

Ingredients

- ½ cup corn kernels
- ¼ cup safflower oil (peanut oil also works fine if you want a flavored oil)
- 3 green onions, diced
- 2 tbsp fresh parsley, choped
- 1 tsp sea salt
- ½ yellow bell pepper, finely chopped
- 1 tsp sesame oil
- 1 celery stalk, finely chopped
- 4 cups brown rice, cooked
- ¼ cup rice vinegar
- 1 carrot, chopped
- ½ cup snow peas, diced
- ½ tsp freshly ground black pepper
- 1 tsp sugar

Method

1. Mix safflower oil, sesame oil, black pepper, salt, and sugar in a small bowl. Mix well until the sugar dissolves into the oil.

2. Add brown rice into a large bowl and pour the oil mixture on it. Toss to coat the rice and let it sit.

3. Steam corn, snow peas, and carrots until they are slightly soft: this should take 2 minutes. Give the veggies an ice bath, then drain and stir them into the rice.

4. Add rice vinegar, celery, green onions, bell pepper, and corn kernels into the bowl and toss.

5. Garnish the salad with parsley. You can serve chilled.

Nutritional Information

Each serving contains:

319 cal | 6g protein | 53g carbs | 4g fiber | 9g fat | 2g sat. fat | 318mg sodium

Chicken Noodle Soup

Prep 15min | cook 2H 15 min

Ingredients

- 2 cups egg noodles
- 2 tbsp vegetable oil
- 1 bay leaf
- 2 medium onions, diced
- 3 sprigs fresh thyme
- 3 medium carrots, thinly chopped
- 4 sprigs fresh parsley plus 1 chopped parsley for garnish
- 3 celery ribs, thinly chopped
- 1 quart cold water
- 1 7-lb chicken
- 2 quarts chicken broth
- Freshly ground black pepper
- Salt

Method

1. Set the stockpot to medium heat and add oil. When the oil gets hot, cook carrots, celery, and onions in it for about 10 minutes or until it's tender.

2. Divide the chicken into 8 parts without removing the fat. Increase the heat of the stockpot to high and add the chicken pieces. Pour in cold water and chicken broth and cook. When foam rises, take them out before they fall off the sides of the pot.

3. Add bay leaf, thyme, and parsley into the pot, then cook on low heat for about 2 hours. This should be enough time for the chicken to soften.

4. Take the chicken out and let it sit until cool enough to handle. Remove the bay leaf, thyme sprigs, and parsley from the pot and throw them in the bin.

5. Degrease your stockpot.

6. Discard the bones and skin of your chicken and mince the meat. Add noodles to the pot and cook for about 10 minutes.

7. Next, add the minced meat to the pot and season with salt and pepper. Stir well and serve.

8. To preserve, set it aside to cool down and keep covered in your refrigerator for 3 months.

Nutritional Information

Each serving contains:

588 cal | 61g protein | 8g carbs | 1g fiber | 33g fat | 9g sat. fat

Strawberry Spinach Salad With Red WineVinaigrette

Prep 10 min | cook 0 min

Ingredients

- 2 cups dried strawberries, hulled
- ½ tsp sesame seeds, toasted
- 6 cups fresh spinach leaves, shredded

For the vinaigrette:

- ⅛ tsp dry mustard
- ¼ cup olive oil
- ⅛ tsp garlic powder
- ½ tsp dried dill weed
- 2 tbsp red wine vinegar
- ⅛ tsp onion powder
- 1 ½ tbsp sugar

Method

1. Add sesame seeds and spinach into a large bowl and mix well.

2. Divide strawberries in two and add them to the spinach. Cover the bowl and keep in the refrigerator.

3. Into a shaker, add olive oil, vinegar, sugar, dill weed, onion powder, garlic powder, and mustard. Shake the jar, cover, and keep it in the refrigerator to cool.

4. Pour the vinaigrette over the spinach mixture and toss.

5. serve.

Nutritional Information

Each serving contains:

114 cal | 4g protein | 13g carbs | 4g fiber | 10g fat | 1g sat. fat | 78mg sodium

Pasta With Caruso Sauce

Prep 10 min | cook 25 min

Ingredients

- ¼ cup Parmesan cheese, shredded
- 1 lb pasta
- ½ cup mozzarella cheese, shredded
- 2 tbsp olive oil
- 2 cup milk
- 1 large onion, diced
- 1 tbsp beef bouillon
- 1 cup mushrooms, sliced
- 3 tbsp flour
- ¼ lb smoked deli ham, diced
- 3 tbsp butter
- Parsley

Method

1. Set your stove to medium heat and place a nonstick skillet on it. Heat olive oil in the pan and sauté the onion until it is tender and fragrant. This should take no more than 5 minutes.

2. Cook mushrooms in the pan and stir occasionally until they turn light brown. Add ham and stir for 2 minutes. Take the pan down and set aside.

3. Now place a large pot containing water on the stove. Add 2 pinches of salt, and cook your pasta according to the directions on the pack.

4. As it cooks, place a saucepan over medium heat and melt butter in it. Add flour and whisk until bubbly.

5. Stir milk into the flour, then add bouillon. Continue stirring until the sauce thickens and almost boils. Take the pan down and add both cheeses and the fried mushroom mixture.

6. Drain your pasta and ladle sauce on it. Garnish with parsley and serve.

Nutritional Information

Each serving contains:

792 cal | 21g protein | 74g carbs | 5g fiber | 47g fat | 25g sat. fat | 897mg sodium

Vegetable Beef Soup

Prep 15 min | cook 3H 15 min

Ingredients

- 2 tbsp parsley, chopped
- 2 tbsp bacon drippings
- ¼ cup long grain rice
- 4 lb beef shanks
- 1 14.5 oz can diced tomatoes
- 2 quarts cold water
- 2 celery stalks, minced
- 1 tsp kosher salt
- 1 lb red skinned potatoes
- ¼ tsp ground black pepper
- ½ lb green beans
- 1 small onion, diced
- 5 peeled carrots, chopped into ¼ inch slices

Method

1. Add bacon drippings into a large stockpot, and heat it over medium heat.

2. Throw in beef shanks and stir while it cooks. When it has turned light brown, add water until it covers the beef. Increase the heat to high and boil.

3. Season with salt and pepper and add diced onions. Reduce the heat to low and simmer for 2 hours.

4. Afterward add rice, carrots, tomatoes, beans, celery, and potatoes into the pot. Cover and simmer for another hour.

5. Discard the bones, then dice the meat. Add chopped meat back into the pot and continue cooking.

6. You can taste the soup to see if you need to adjust the seasonings.

7. Add parsley, stir well, and serve.

Nutritional Information

Each serving contains:

453 cal | 64g protein | 16g carbs | 3g fiber | 13g fat | 5g sat. fat | 443mg sodium

Honeyed Fruit Salad

Prep 15 min | cook 0 min

Ingredients

- 2 tbsp parsley, chopped
- ¾ cup sweet cherries, pitted
- ½ cup dry white wine
- 2 peaches, pitted
- 4 tbsp honey
- 2 tbsp lemon juice
- 2 pears, cored
- ½ tsp lemon zest
- 1 pint strawberries, hulled
- 1 tbsp sugar
- 1 kiwi

Method

1. Add wine, honey, lemon juice, zest, and sugar into a blender, and process until you get a smooth consistency.

2. Keep the dressing in a bowl, cover, and refrigerate for 20 minutes.

3. Divide strawberries into two parts and chop both pears and peaches into ¾ inch bits. Also, halve the kiwi and cherries and add these fruits to the dressing.

4. Toss and serve chilled.

Nutritional Information

Each serving contains:

121 cal | 1g protein | 29g carbs | 4g fiber | 0g fat | 0g sat. fat | 2mg sodium

Chicken Waldorf Sandwiches

Prep 20 min | cook 0 min

Ingredients	Method
•Butter lettuce •2 12-oz cans chicken, drained •8 slices cinnamon raisin bread •2 unpeeled Granny Smith apples, chopped •2 tsp lemon juice •1 cup chopped celery •2 tbsp honey mustard •½ cup walnuts, diced •2 tbsp plain yogurt •½ cup dried cranberries •½ cup mayonnaise •Pinch salt	1. Into a medium-sized bowl, add walnuts, apples, lemon juice, yogurt, salt, mustard, cranberries, chicken, and celery. Toss well to combine. 2. Place lettuce on bread, add the chicken mixture, and cover with another bread slice to make the sandwich. 3. Seal in an airtight container. Chicken Waldorf Sandwiches can be stored in a refrigerator for 2 days. Nutritional Information Each sandwich contains: 540 cal | 34g protein | 20g carbs | 4g fiber | 36g fat | 7g sat. fat | 338mg sodium

Easy Banana Muffins

Prep 5 min | cook 25 min

Ingredients

- 1 tsp baking soda
- 4 ripe bananas
- 1 tsp salt
- ¼ cup oil
- 2 cups all-purpose flour
- 1 cup organic sugar
- 1 cup walnuts, diced

Method

1. Make sure your oven is preheated to 360°F and oil a 12-cup muffin tin with nonstick cooking spray.

2. Place the bananas in a large bowl and mash them with a fork.

3. Add sugar and oil to the bananas and mix well to form cream.

4. Add baking soda, flour, and salt to a medium-sized bowl and combine. Transfer this mixture to the large bowl and stir gently to form a thick batter.

5. Using a spoon, add the batter to the muffin cups. They should be filled 2/3 of the way. Sprinkle with walnuts.

6. Pop the muffin tin in the oven to bake for about 25 minutes. A toothpick inserted at the center of any muffin should come out clean.

7. Let it sit for a while to cool down, then serve.

Nutritional Information

Each muffin contains:

218 cal | 3g protein | 32g carbs | 2g fiber | 10g fat | 1g sat. fat | 253mg sodium

Potato and Ham Soup With Cheese

Prep 15min | cook 30 min

Ingredients

- 1 cup cooked ham, cut into 4 parts
- 3 medium red potatoes, peeled and cubed
- 1 cup cheddar cheese, shredded
- 2 cups water
- 3 cups milk
- ¼ tsp salt
- 3 tbsp all-purpose flour
- ¼ cup onion, diced
- 3 tbsp butter
- Freshly ground black pepper
- 2 tbsp chopped parsley

Method

1. Set stove to medium-high heat. Pour water into a pot, add salt, and boil.

2. Cook the potatoes in the pot until considerably softer.

3. Drain the pot, but set aside 1 cup of the potato water.

4. Reduce the stove to medium heat and place a saucepan on it. Melt butter in the pan and add onions. Sauté until tender.

5. Stir the flour into the pan until you have a well combined and smooth mixture.

6. Add black pepper and stir for about 1 minute. Pour the potato water and milk into the pan. Stir well and add potatoes. Also, add ham and cheese

7. Reduce the heat to low, top with parsley, and stir occasionally for about 20 minutes.

8. Serve.

Nutritional Information

Each serving contains:

310 cal | 13g protein | 22g carbs | 2g fiber | 19g fat | 11g sat. fat | 535mg sodium

Vegetable Fried Rice With Spinach

Prep 10 min | cook 8 min

Ingredients

- ½ lime, juiced
- 3 garlic cloves, thinly chopped
- 1/3 tsp sea salt
- 3 tbsp extra virgin olive oil
- 1 tbsp sesame oil
- 2 cups cooked rice
- ¼ cup soy sauce
- 1 tomato, diced
- ½ cup green beans
- 1 cup chopped spinach

Method

1. Set stove to medium heat and place a saucepan containing oil on it. Add garlic into the pan and sauté for about 2 minutes.

2. Stir in tomatoes, spinach, green beans, soy sauce, sesame oil, and cooked rice. Let this cook for 8 minutes and stir occasionally.

3. Turn the stove off and take the pan down. Stir in lime juice and sea salt, then serve.

Nutritional Information

Each serving contains:

814 cal | 21g protein | 139g carbs | 20g fat | 3g sat. fat | 1588mg sodium

Horiatiki Salata

Prep 15 min | cook 0 min

Ingredients	Method
• 1 tbsp water • 5 large ripe tomatoes, cored and diced • 12 Greek olives • 1 cucumber, minced • Pepper • 1 green bell pepper, remove seeds and stem and cut into rings • ¼ lb feta cheese, shredded • 1 large red onion, thinly sliced • Extra virgin olive oil • Sea salt • Dried Greek oregano • Sea salt	1. Add bell pepper, onions, cucumbers, and green pepper into a large salad bowl. Add salt and mix well. Also, add oil and oregano, and toss. 2. Top with cheese, pepper, and Greek olives. Toss well. 3. Serve. Nutritional Information Each serving contains: 86 cal	4g protein	7g carbs	2g fiber	5g fat	3g sat. fat	292mg sodium

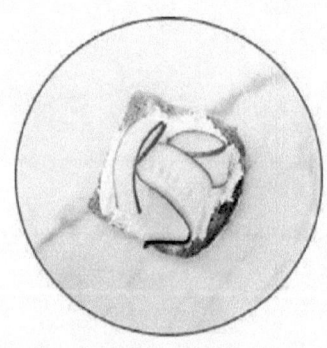

Cucumber Cream Cheese Tea Sandwiches

Prep 15 min | cook 0 min

Ingredients

- Lemon juice
- 1 loaf buttermilk bread
- 1 English cucumber, minced
- ½ cup cream cheese
- Pepper
- Salt
- Fresh chives, chopped

Method

1. Spread cream cheese on one side of two slices of bread.

2. Cover one slice with cucumbers, and add lemon juice, chives, pepper, and salt.

3. Make into the sandwich by covering with the other bread slice.

4. Remove the bread crusts and slice the sandwich diagonally. This way, you create four small triangles.

5. Repeat with the other ingredients and serve.

Nutritional Information

Each sandwich contains:

36 cal | 1g protein | 1g carbs | 0 fiber | 3g fat | 2g sat. fat | 41mg sodium

Macaroni and Cheese Casserole
With Ground Beef

Prep 18 min | cook 50 min

Ingredients

- 2 cups cheddar cheese, shredded
- 8 oz elbow macaroni
- 14.5 oz stewed tomatoes
- ¼ cup onion, diced
- 1 medium bay leaf
- 1 medium green pepper, chopped
- 1 lb ground beef
- 1 garlic clove, chopped
- ½ tsp pepper
- ¼ cup butter
- Salt

Method

1. Cook the macaroni according to the directions on the pack. Drain.

2. Preheat the oven to 350°F and prepare a 2-quart baking dish by coating it with butter.

3. Put the beef, ¼ tsp salt, pepper, onion, butter, green pepper, and garlic into a large saucepan.

4. Set stove to medium-high heat and cook the contents of the saucepan for about 2 minutes. Reduce the heat to low and add tomatoes and bay leaf. Cook for about 17 minutes. Stir in 1 ½ cups of cheese for 1 minute.

5. Using a spoon, add ½ of the cooked macaroni to the baking dish. Add the beef mixture, and follow this with the remaining ½ macaroni.

6. Sprinkle with ½ cup of cheese and bake open for 30 minutes.

7. Take the baking dish out and let it sit to cool down.

8. Serve.

Nutritional Information

Each serving contains:

665 cal | 44g protein | 24g carbs | 3g fiber | 44g fat | 24g sat.

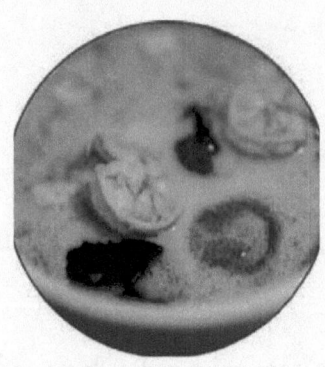

Slow Cooker Taco Soup

Prep 5 min | cook 0 min

Ingredients

- ½ tsp garlic powder
- 14 oz can corn, drained
- ½ tsp salt
- 14 oz can kidney beans, drained
- ¾ tsp onion powder
- 14 oz can pinto beans, drained
- ¼ tsp cumin
- 14 oz can black beans, drained
- 1 oz pack taco seasoning mix
- 14 oz can Mexican-style stewed tomatoes, undrained

For garnish:

- Sour cream
- Tortilla chips
- Fresh cilantro, diced
- Cheddar cheese, grated

Method

1. Into a crockpot, add stewed tomatoes, drained corn, black beans, kidney beans, and pinto beans. Stir well.

2. Add garlic powder, cumin taco mix, salt, and onion powder into the pot, and stir again.

3. Set the crockpot to low and cook for about 8 hours: this means that you should cook this meal a day before. If you want to get this one faster, however, set the pot to high and cook for 3 hours.

4. Give it a quick taste and adjust the seasoning if necessary.

5. If the soup is not thick enough, continue cooking. You can also adjust thickness with vegetable broth.

6. Serve in small bowls and top with preferred garnishes.

Nutritional Information

Each serving contains:

1126 cal | 53g protein | 203 carbs | 41g fiber | 14g fat | 2g sat. fat | 200mg sodium

Tomato Soup

Prep 15 min | cook 26 min

Ingredients	Method
• 2 tbsp tomato paste	1. Set stove to medium heat and place a large pot containing oil on it.
• 1 tbsp olive oil	
• 1 cup chicken broth	2. Sauté your onions in the hot oil for about 3 minutes, then add garlic and carrots. Sauté for 3 extra minutes.
• 1 onion, diced	
• 28 oz can crushed tomatoes	3. Add both crushed and diced tomatoes into the pot. Also, add tomato paste and chicken broth. Reduce the heat to medium-low and cook for 20 minutes with the pot open.
• 1 large carrot, peeled and diced	
• 2 large tomatoes, seeded and chopped	4. Use an immersion blender to mix the soup while in the pot or transfer to a food processor. Purée until you achieve a smooth consistency. Be careful while doing this, as the soup is hot and can cause burns.
• 2 garlic cloves, thinly chopped	
• Kosher salt to desired taste	Nutritional Information
• Freshly ground black pepper to desired taste	Each serving contains:
	172 cal	6g protein	31g carbs	6g fiber	4g fat	1g sat. fat	303mg sodium

Caprese Salad

Prep 10 min | cook 0 min

Ingredients

- ¼ cup olive oil
- 4 large heirloom tomatoes, chopped into ¼ inch slices
- 12 fresh basil leaves
- 8 oz fresh mozzarella cheese, diced into ¼ inch slices
- 1/3 cup lemon juice
- Salt and pepper to preferred taste
- For the glaze:
- 2 tbsp sugar
- 1 cup balsamic vinegar

Method

To prepare the balsamic glaze:

1. Add sugar and balsamic vinegar into a saucepan and whisk well. Set stove to medium-low heat and place the pan on it for about 10 minutes. Stir occasionally until the mixture thickens.

To prepare the salad:

1. Salt the diced tomatoes to the desired taste.

2. Into a small flat plate, place one slice of the salted tomatoes. Top with two basil leaves and a slice of cheese.

3. Continue layering tomato slices, basil, and cheese in this order until the plate is filled. Pour olive oil over these ingredients and season with salt and pepper.

4. Pour the lemon juice and balsamic glaze over the salad, and serve.

Nutritional Information

Each serving contains:

218 cal | 7g protein | 3g carbs | 1g fiber | 20g fat | 6g sat. fat | 268mg sodium

Chicken Salad With Grapes

Prep 15 min | cook 0 min

Ingredients

- 12 red seedless grapes, divided into two
- 1 ½ cups skinless chicken, cooked and cubed
- Salt to desired taste
- ½ cup celery, chopped
- Freshly ground black pepper to desired taste
- 1 scallion, thinly sliced
- 4 tbsp mayonnaise
- ⅛ tsp curry powder
- Grape tomatoes, halved
- Chopped nuts, toasted
- Lettuce

Method

1. Add cubed chicken, celery, and scallion into a large bowl. Also, add 3 tbsp of mayonnaise and toss.

2. Season with pepper and salt. You can add more mayonnaise if you desire.

3. Throw in grapes, tomatoes, curry powder, and nuts. Mix well to combine.

4. Spread lettuce leaves on a flat plate and add the chicken salad. Serve.

Nutritional Information

Each serving contains:

620 cal | 36g protein | 65g carbs | 4g fiber | 26g fat | 6g sat. fat | 257mg sodium

Cold Soba Noodle Salad

Prep 15 min | cook 5 min

Ingredients	Method
• 1 tbsp sesame seeds • 8 oz dried soba noodles • 2 tbsp fresh cilantro, diced • 2 tbsp canola oil • 4 spring onions, diced • 1 lime juice • 6 small radishes, minced • 1 tbsp fresh ginger, grated • 1 small red bell pepper, minced • 1 tbsp rice wine vinegar • 2 medium carrots, shredded • 1 tsp sesame oil • 4 small Persian cucumbers, minced • 1 tsp honey • ⅛ tsp salt and pepper	1. Prepare the noodles according to the directions on the pack. Rinse with cold water, drain, and set aside 2. Into a small mixing bowl, add Sriracha, canola oil, sesame oil honey, lime juice, vinegar, and ginger. Stir in salt and pepper. 3. In a separate large bowl, add noodles, cilantro, cucumber, onion, carrot, radish, and bell pepper. Transfer the dressing into this bowl and toss. Taste to see if seasoning should be adjusted. 4. Serve immediately with sesame seed toppings. You can preserve this salad in your refrigerator for one day. Nutritional Information Each serving contains: 324 cal | 7g protein | 47g carbs | 5g fiber | 13g fat | 1g sat. fat | 758m sodium

Mac and Cheese Muffins

Prep 5 min | cook 35 min

Ingredients

- ⅛ cup cayenne pepper
- 1 lb elbow macaroni
- 3 slices provolone, scattered
- 6 tbsp unsalted butter
- 1 cup mozzarella cheese, grated
- 2 tbsp all-purpose flour
- 1 cup sharp cheddar cheese, grated
- 12 oz can evaporated milk
- 1 cup Jack cheese, grated
- 2 ½ cups whole milk
- 1 tbsp Dijon mustard
- Kosher salt to desired taste

Method

1. Make sure your oven is preheated to 375°F. Prepare two 12-cup muffin pans by coating them with nonstick cooking spray.

2. Set your stove to medium-high heat and place a large pot containing water on it. When the water begins to boil, cook the pasta according to the directions on the pack.

3. Drain the macaroni, but reserve ¾ of the cooking liquid.

4. Place the pot back on the stove and melt butter in it. Add flour and stir for about 2 minutes. Add both milks and reserved cooking water into the pot and stir. When it thickens, put in salt, mustard, and cheeses. Mix well until the cheeses melt.

5. Add cayenne and macaroni to the mixture in the pot. Stir until well incorporated, then add into the muffin cups. Make sure the cups are filled, then pop in the oven for about 20 minutes.

6. Take out the pan and set aside to cool down. Transfer to a wire rack to cool completely. This should take no more than 5 minutes.

7. Serve hot.

Nutritional Information

Each serving contains:

197 cal | 9g protein | 11g carbs | 1g fiber | 13g fat | 8g sat. fat | 299mg sodium

Crispy Chicken Tenders

Prep 20 min | cook 15 min

Ingredients

- 1 lb free-range chicken tenders
- 2 cups panko breadcrumbs
- ½ cup all-purpose flour
- 1 tbsp ground turmeric
- 2 large eggs
- 2 tsp cayenne pepper
- 2 tsp kosher salt
- 2 tsp freshly ground black pepper
- Mustard Dressing
- 2 tbsp runny honey
- 4 tbsp mustard
- 4 tbsp vegetable oil

Method

1. Make sure your oven is preheated to 425°F.

2. Place cayenne, breadcrumbs, salt, turmeric, and black pepper into a large bowl. Mix well and add to a baking sheet. Toast crumbs in the oven for about 5 minutes, then add to a shallow plate.

3. Crack eggs into a medium-sized bowl and add flour to a shallow plate.

4. Using tongs or any appropriate kitchen utensil, coat a chicken tender in the flour and shake off any excess.

5. Next, dip the floured tender in the egg and shake again to remove excess.

6. Press the chicken tender in the breadcrumbs and roll it to coat all sides. Again, shake the tender gently.

7. Place the coated chicken tenders on a grill pan and pop in the center of the oven to bake for 7 minutes. You might need a second pan.

8. Flip and bake for another 7 minutes. A temperature probe should read 165F when placed on the chicken tenders.

9. Add mustard, runny honey, and vegetable oil into a screw top jar, and shake well until thick and creamy. Add salt and pepper as desired.

10. Serve the tenders in a small flat plate, with dressing in a separate small bowl.

Nutritional Information

Each serving contains:

896 cal | 73g protein | 38g carbs | 3g fiber | 48g fat | 12g sat.

Greek Mini Frittatas

Prep 20 min | cook 15 min

Ingredients

- ¾ cup feta cheese, shredded
- 2 tbsp unsalted butter
- 8 extra-large eggs
- 1 cup onion, diced
- ½ tsp dried thyme
- 1 cup red bell pepper, diced
- ½ tsp dried oregano
- Kosher salt to desired taste
- 2 cup mushrooms, diced
- Black pepper to preferred taste
- Nonstick cooking spray

Method

1. Make sure the oven is preheated to 350°F, and prepare a 12-cup muffin pan by oiling it with cooking spray.

2. Set your stove to medium heat and place a skillet containing 1 tbsp butter on it.

3. After the butter melts, add bell pepper and onion into the skillet. Also, stir in salt and pepper and cook for 6 minutes.

4. Transfer the now tender onions and red pepper to a small plate and increase the heat to medium-high.

5. Melt another 1 tbsp of butter in the same pan and add thyme, oregano, and mushrooms. Add salt and pepper and sauté until the mushrooms turn light brown.

6. Place the mushrooms on the same plate as the onions and pepper.

7. Crack eggs into a medium-sized bowl and whisk. Add the mushroom mixture to the eggs and stir well.

8. Spoon the egg and veggie mixture into the muffin cups and sprinkle with cheese.

9. Bake in the preheated oven for about 2 minutes, then remove the frittatas with the aid of a butter knife.

10. Serve.

Nutritional Information :

Each frittata contains:

109 cal | 7g protein | 4g carbs | 1g fiber | 8g fat | 4g sat. fat | 221mg sodium

Spinach Cashew Pesto

Prep 5 min | cook 0 mi

Ingredients

- ½ cup extra virgin olive oil
- 2 cups baby spinach, stem discarded
- 1 tsp sea salt
- 2 cups fresh sweet basil
- 1 ½ cups ground cashew
- 4 large garlic cloves, minced
- ¼ cup nutritional yeast

Method

1. Into a food processor, add cashews, spinach, lemon juice, basil, nutritional yeast, salt, and garlic. Purée until you get a chunky consistency. This might take 30 seconds.

2. Add oil to the food processor and blend for another 30 seconds.

3. Enjoy.

Nutritional Information

Each serving contains:

46 cal | 2g protein | 5g carbs | 3g fiber | 3g fat | 1g sat. fat | 136mg sodium

Crock Pot Hamburger Soup

Prep 15 min | cook 8 H

Ingredients

- 1 cup macaroni
- 1 lb ground beef
- ½ cup fresh parsley, chopped
- 1 onion, chopped
- 1 tbsp soy sauce
- 16 oz pack mixed vegetables, frozen
- 1 tbsp salt
- 3 ribs celery, diced
- 1 bay leaf
- 14.5 oz can beef broth
- ½ tsp paprika
- 1 green pepper, diced
- 2 sprigs fresh thyme
- 1 envelope dry onion soup mix
- 2 tbsp fresh basil, chopped
- 8 oz can tomato sauce
- 2 tbsp fresh oregano, chopped
- ¼ cup barley

Method

1. Set stove to medium-high heat and place a sauté pan on it. Add ground beef to the pan and brown. Transfer the beef to a colander and pour hot water on it to get rid of excess fat.

2. Place beef and every ingredient on the list inside a slow cooker, and add water to almost fill the pot. An inch to the top of the crockpot should be free of water.

3. Set the pot to low and cook for 8 hours. You can also set the cooker to high and cook for half the time.

4. Cook macaroni according to the directions on the pack, then add to the pot. This should be done 30 minutes before you serve the meal.

Nutritional Information

Each serving contains:

417 cal | 33g protein | 47g carbs | 9g fiber | 11g fat | 4g sat. fat | 1728mg sodium

Tofu and Egg Salad

Prep 10 min | cook 10 min

Ingredients

- 1 tbsp mustard
- 14 oz block firm tofu, drain
- ½ tsp onion powder
- 1/3 cup vegan mayonnaise
- ½ tsp garlic powder
- 1/3 cup sweet pickle relish
- ½ stalk celery, chopped
- ½ tsp lemon juice
- ⅛ paprika

Method

1. Add tofu into a medium-sized bowl and mash with a fork. You can leave it a little crumbly.

2. Add celery, lemon juice, mayonnaise, garlic powder, mustard, onion powder, and pickle relish to the tofu. Mix well.

3. Adjust seasonings to your preference.

4. For the garnish, sprinkle with paprika. Serve.

Nutritional Information

Each serving contains:

269 cal | 12g protein | 12g carbs | 2g fiber | 21g fat | 3g sat. fat | 357mg sodium

Chapter 6: Snacking Like a Boss

Snacks often get a bad rap for being unhealthy or a needless addition to a person's diet. However, neither of these are categorically true. Snacks can be healthy and they are also important.

Regardless of the nature of what you consume, if it's digestible, then it provides the body with some level of energy. When that energy is depleted, we may feel tired and grumpy. Should your kids experience this 'low' when they need to be upbeat and productive, a quick snack might just be the solution.

Snacks are great because they often require little to no cooking or preparation; plus, they're almost always fun to eat. You should treat your kids to the lovely snacks listed below.

Sweet Spinach Muffins

Prep 10 min | cook 22 min

Ingredients

- 1 tsp vanilla extract
- 18 cupcake liners
- 1 large egg
- 2 cup whole wheat flour
- 6 oz raw baby spinach
- 1 ½ tsp cinnamon
- 1 large banana
- 2 tsp baking powder
- ½ cup honey
- ½ tsp baking soda
- ¾ cup milk
- ¼ tsp salt
- ½ cup unsalted butter, melted

Method

1. Make sure your oven is preheated to 350°F. Prepare a muffin pan by covering it with paper liners.

2. Into a large mixing bowl, add flour, cinnamon, baking powder, baking soda, and salt. Combine.

3. Add melted butter, honey, vanilla, raw spinach, milk, banana, and egg into a food processor and blend.

4. Pour this purée into the bowl containing the flour mixture, and fold until well combined.

5. Using a spoon, transfer the batter into the muffin pan and bake for 22 minutes. This should be time enough for the muffins to toughen, without turning brown.

6. Set aside to cool, then serve.

Nutritional Information

Each serving contains:

139 cal | 3g protein | 20g carbs | 2g fiber | 6g fat | 4g sat. fat | 85mg sodium

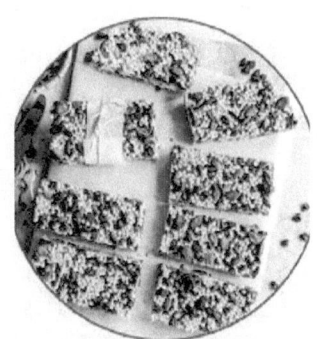

No-Bake Date Bar

Prep 35 min | cook 0 min

Ingredients

- 2 tbsp cocoa powder
- 2 cup dates, pitted
- ½ cup coconut flakes
- ¾ cup cashews
- ¼ cup peanut butter
- Pinch salt

Method

1. Make sure your oven is preheated to 350°F. Prepare a
1. Add all the ingredients on the list into a food processor and blend until they form into a smooth ball.

2. Line a 9-inch square baking dish with parchment paper, and place the mixture on it.

3. Using clean hands, press down on the ball. Then cover the pan and place in the oven for about 30 minutes.

4. Remove from the oven and divide into 9 small bars.

5. Enjoy right away or seal up in an airtight container and refrigerate.

Nutritional Information

Each bar contains:

265 cal | 5g protein | 45g carbs | 5g fiber | 10g fat | 3g sat. fat | 79mg sodium

Homemade Teething

Prep 35 min | cook 0 min

Ingredients

- 2 tbsp coconut oil
- 2 cups dry oats
- 1 medium banana
- ⅛ tsp cinnamon
- 1 tsp vanilla extract

Method

1. Add all the ingredients on the list into a food 1.Make sure your oven is preheated to 350°F. Also, prepare a baking sheet by lining it with parchment paper.

2. Using a blender, grind the oats into a smooth powder. Add coconut oil and banana to the ground oats in the blender and process some more. The mixture should clump into dough now.

3. Pour a little more coconut oil on the dough if it is too dry. Coat with wheat flour if the dough sticks to your fingers.

4. Make 12 small balls out of the dough. Roll out the small balls until they are ¼ inch thick, 4 inches long, and 1 ½ inch wide. Make it into a flat round shape by curving out the edges with your fingers.

5. Place them on the baking sheet, but ensure that they don't touch themselves. Bake for about 10 minutes, flip, and cook for an additional 10 minutes.

6. The edges of the biscuits should be slightly brown and the center should no longer be runny. Make sure it isn't too crunchy.

7. Set aside to cool completely. Serve.

Nutritional Information

Each biscuit contains:

394 cal | 14g protein | 50g carbs | 9g fiber | 12g fat | 7g sat. fat | 2mg sodium

Zucchini Oat Muffins

Pre 15 min | cook 20 min

Ingredients

- ½ cup dry oats
- 1 ½ cup whole wheat flour
- 1 ½ cup zucchini, peeled and grated
- 1 tsp baking powder
- 1 tsp vanilla extract
- 1 tsp baking soda
- 1/3 cup coconut oil
- 1 tsp cinnamon
- 1/3 cup unsweetened almond milk
- ½ tsp salt
- ½ cup pure maple syrup
- 1 large egg
- Nonstick cooking spray

Method

1. Make sure your oven preheats to 350°F. Also, prepare a 12-cup muffin tin by oiling it with cooking spray.

2. Add soda, flour, cinnamon, baking powder, and salt into a large bowl and whisk well.

3. Make a hole at the center of the flour mixture and crack an egg into it. Also, add vanilla, maple syrup, coconut oil, honey, and milk. Mix, but only slightly. Stir in oats and shredded oats.

4. Spoon this mixture into the muffin cups. If you prefer, top with some more oats. Pop in the oven to bake for about 20 minutes. A toothpick pushed into the center of each muffin should come out clean.

5. Set aside for about 3 minutes to cool down a little, then transfer to a wire rack for 5 minutes.

6. Serve warm.

Nutritional Information

Each muffin contains:

177 cal | 4g protein | 25g carbs | 3g fiber | 7g fat | 5g sat. fat | 218mg sodium

Banana Bread

Prep 15 min | cook 55 min

Ingredients

- ½ cup walnuts, diced
- 1 cup whole wheat flour
- 1 tsp vanilla extract
- 1 cup white whole-wheat flour
- 2 large eggs
- 1 tsp baking soda
- ½ cup plain yogurt
- ¼ tsp salt
- 6 tbsp butter
- 4 bananas, mashed
- ¼ cup honey
- Nonstick cooking spray

Method

a loaf pan by coating it with cooking spray.

2. Add baking soda, flour, baking powder, and salt into a medium-sized bowl, and mix well. Set the bowl aside.

3. Set your stove to medium-high heat and place a saucepan containing butter on it. Melt the butter and stir in mashed banana, honey, vanilla, and yogurt.

4. Take the pan down and let the mixture cool slightly. This should be no more than 30 seconds. Crack eggs in and mix. Return pan to the stove.

5. Stir in baking powder mixture and ¼ cup walnuts. Mix until well combined.

6. Transfer this mixture to the prepared loaf pan and top with the remaining walnuts.

7. Pop in the oven and bake for about 55 minutes. A toothpick pushed into the center of the bread should come out unstained.

8. Take the pan out of the oven and set aside for 10 minutes. Transfer to a wire rack to cool down completely.

Nutritional Information

Makes 8 slices

Each bread slice contains:
318 cal | 8g protein | 42g carbs | 5g fiber | 15g fat | 6g sat. fat | 246mg sodium

Strawberry Watermelon Smoothie

Prep 5 min | cook 0 min

Ingredients	Method
•4 cups strawberries, frozen •4 cups cubed watermelon	1. Thaw strawberries and place them in a blender. Add watermelon and blend until you get a smooth mixture. 2. Serve. Nutritional Information Makes 4 servings Each serving contains: 72 cal | 1g protein | 18g carbs | 2g fiber | 0g fat | 0g sat. fat | 3mg sodium

Whipped Pineapple Pops

Prep 10min | cook 3H FREEZE

Ingredients

- 1 ½ cup heavy whipping cream
- 1 medium lime, juiced
- 5 cups pineapple

Method

1. Add pineapples and lime juice to a blender, and mix until you get a smooth consistency.

2. Pour in cream and blend some more. Transfer mixture to 8 popsicle molds and keep in the freezer for 3 hours, or until hardened.

3. Serve.

Nutritional Information

Each popsicle contains:

206 cal | 2g protein | 16g carbs | 2g fiber | 16g fat | 10g sat. fat| 13mg sodium

Slow Cooker Applesauce

Prep 15 min | cook 4H 15 min

Ingredients

- ½ cup water
- 8 medium apples, diced
- Vanilla bean
- 3 cinnamon sticks

Method

1. Place apple slices into a slow cooker and add water, vanilla bean, and cinnamon sticks.

2. Set the cooker to low and cook the apple mixture for about 4 hours.

3. The apples should be considerably tender now. You can just stir well and serve chunky applesauce.

4. Otherwise, discard bean and cinnamon sticks, and transfer apple slices to a blender, and puree until smooth.

5. Serve or store in glass mason jars. This applesauce can be preserved in a refrigerator for up to one week.

Nutritional Information

Makes 4 servings

Each serving contains:

241 cal | 1g protein | 64g carbs | 12g fiber | 1g fat | 0g sat. fat | 6mg sodium

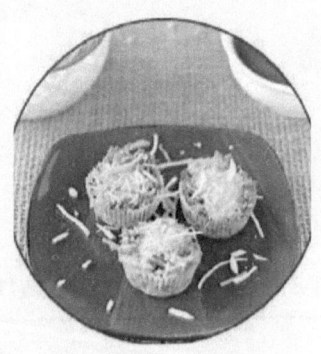

Quinoa Pizza Bites

Prep 20 min | cook 30 min

Ingredients

- Parmesan cheese, grated
- Fresh basil
- 1 cup cooked quinoa, cooled
- ½ tsp pepper
- 2 cups cooked cauliflower florets, cooled and pureed
- 2 tbsp pizza sauce, extra for dipping
- 1 egg
- 1 ½ tsp sea salt
- ¼ cup white rice flour
- 2 tsp Italian seasoning
- 2 tbsp coconut flour
- 1 ½ tsp garlic powder
- 2 tsp onion powder

Method

1. Make sure to preheat your oven to 400°F.

2. Add every ingredient on the list to a small bowl and mix well. Roll this mixture into 24 small balls.

3. Line a baking sheet with parchment paper, then add the balls into the pan. Place the baking sheet in the oven and bake for 30 minutes.

4. For garnishing, top with cheese and basil. Serve with extra pizza sauce as dipping.

Nutritional Information

Each pizza bite contains:

286 cal | 12g protein | 45g carbs | 5g fiber | 7g fat | 2g sat. fat | 1128mg sodium

Banana Roll-Ups

Prep 10 min | cook 5 min

Ingredients

- 3 medium whole wheat tortillas
- ½ cup cream cheese, low-fat
- 3 medium banana
- 2 tsp honey
- ¼ tsp cinnamon

Method

1. Into a small bowl, add honey, cream cheese, and cinnamon. Mix until smooth, then lather on each tortilla.

2. Wrap each banana in the tortillas and transfer to a hot griddle. Cook until golden brown.

3. Slice the roll-ups to make 8 servings, and serve.

Nutritional Information

Each serving contains:

123 cal | 3g protein | 20g carbs | 3g fiber | 4g fat | 2g sat. fat | 133mg sodium

Parmesan Sweet Potato Zucchini Tots

Prep 25 min | cook 45 min

Ingredients

- 1 medium sweet potato, peeled
- Pinch garlic powder
- 1 medium zucchini
- ¼ tsp paprika
- ¼ cup Parmesan cheese
- ½ tsp sea salt
- Optional creamy ketchup

Method

1. Make sure the oven is preheated to 375F. Line a baking sheet using parchment paper.

2. Set the microwave to high and place the potato in it. Cook for 4 minutes. Take the potato and let it sit for 5-10 minutes to cool down.

3. Grate the potato into a small mixing bowl. Lay a thick paper towel on a clean kitchen surface. Peel the zucchini and grate it onto the paper towel.

4. Juice the shredded zucchini and add the vegetable into the small bowl containing the grated potato.

5. Also, add flour, cheese, garlic powder, sea salt, and paprika to the bowl. Using clean hands, thoroughly mix these ingredients.

6. Mold this mixture into short, thick rods. It should be about 1 ½ inches long.

7. Place the potato tots on the prepared baking sheet. But make sure there is some space between them.

8. Place the pan in the oven and bake for about 20 minutes. Turn them over and bake for an additional 20 minutes. It should turn light brown.

9. Serve hot with the dipping sauce.
To make the creamy ketchup:
1. Add ketchup and Greek yogurt into a small bowl and mix well.

Nutritional Information

Each serving contains:

85 cal | 4g protein | 12g carbs | 2g fiber | 3g fat | 1g sat. fat | 505mg sodium

Strawberry Kiwi Gummies

Prep 2H | cook 3 min

Ingredients

- 2 pack unsweetened gelatin
- 2 cup unsweetened strawberries frozen
- 6 tbsp sugar
- 2 medium kiwi, peeled and diced

Method

1. Place kiwi and strawberries in a small bowl. Add ¼ cup of sugar and set the bowl aside for the strawberries to thaw.

2. Using a fork, mash the fruits in the bowl. Sieve with a cheesecloth, and pour the juice into a saucepan. Discard the solid remains.

3. Stir in the remaining sugar and add gelatin. Whisk well.

4. Set your stove to medium-high heat and place the saucepan containing gelatin mixture on it. Allow to cook for 3 minutes and stir occasionally.

5. Transfer this mixture from the pan into an 8 inch square baking dish. Keep in the refrigerator for about 1 hour.

6. Cut into preferred shapes and enjoy. Gummies can be kept in an airtight container and refrigerated for two weeks.

Nutritional Information

Each gummy contains:

167 cal | 13g protein | 31g carbs | 3g fiber | 0g fat | 0g sat. fat | 30mg sodium

Kettle Corn

Prep 5 min | cook 15 min

Ingredients

- ½ cup popcorn kernels, unpopped
- ¼ cup vegetable oil
- ¼ cup white sugar

Method

1. Set your stove to medium heat and place a large pot containing oil on it. Heat the oil and stir in popcorn and sugar.

2. Cover the pot and cook until the popping only happens once in 3 seconds. You might need to gently shake the pot occasionally to prevent the sugar from burning.

3. Turn off the stove and set the pot down. Shake until you no longer hear that popping sound.

4. Transfer to a large bowl and leave to cool. Stir well to break the clumps.

Nutritional Information

Each Serving contains:

209.3 cal | 2.4g protein | 24.8g carbs | 2.9g fiber | 11.9g fat | 1.8g sat. fat | 0mg sodium

Red Ants on a Log

Prep 5 min | cook 0 min

Ingredients

- 10 dried cranberries
- 1 tbsp peanut butter
- 1 celery stalk

Method

1. Add peanut butter to the groove of the celery and line cranberries on the peanut butter. There should be some space between the cranberries.

Nutritional Information

Each serving contains:

132 cal | 4.4g protein | 12.6g carbs | 0g fiber | 8.3g fat | 1.7g sat. fat | 106.6mg sodium

Potato Cakes

Prep 10 min | cook 10 min

Ingredients

- ½ cup vegetable oil
- 2 cups mashed potatoes
- ½ tsp salt
- 1 cup all-purpose flour
- ½ tsp ground black pepper
- 1 chopped onion
- 1 egg

Method

1. Crack egg into a medium sized bowl. Add mashed potatoes, pepper, flour, salt, onion and mix well into batter.

2. Set stove to medium heat and place the skillet containing oil on it. Using a spoon, take from the batter, and add to the oil. They should be 4 inches in size.

3. Cook both sides of each batter for 5 minutes. Take them out and place them on paper towels to drain.

4. Repeat with what remains of the batter.

Nutritional Information

Each potato cake contains:

254.8 cal | 7.1g protein | 45.1g carbs | 3g fiber | 4.9g fat | 1.1g sat. fat | 627.1mg sodium

Fresh Fruit and Yogurt Ice Pops

Prep 15 min | cook 5H FREEZING

Ingredients

- 8 popsicle sticks
- 2 cups mixed fresh fruits (blueberries, bananas, strawberries, and raspberries), diced
- 8 small paper cups
- 2 cups vanilla yogurt
- ¼ cup white sugar

Method

1. Place mixed fruits into a blender and add sugar. Cover and purée until you get a smooth mixture.

2. Gather the paper cups and add blended fruit mix into them. They should be filled ¾ of the way. Using aluminum foil, cover the cups. Pass popsicle sticks through the foil.

3. Allow to freeze for at least 5 hours.

4. Take off the foil and paper cup, and serve.

Nutritional Information

Each popsicle contains:

83 cal | 3.5g protein | 15.8g carbs | 0.9g fiber | 1.1g fat | 0.6g sat. fat | 43.2mg sodium

Chunky Monkey Pancakes

Prep 10 min | cook 20 min

Ingredients

- ¼ cup pecans, diced
- 1 cup all-purpose flour
- ½ cup semi-sweet chocolate chips
- 2 tsp baking powder
- 1 large banana, chopped
- 1 tsp baking soda
- 1 tsp vanilla extract
- ¼ tsp salt
- 1 tbsp white sugar
- ¾ cup skim milk
- 2 eggs
- 3 tbsp melted butter

Method

1. Place baking powder, baking soda, flour, and salt into a large bowl. Mix well and set aside.

2. Crack eggs into a medium-sized bowl and add milk, vanilla, butter, and eggs.

3. Make a small hole at the center of the flour mixture and pour in the egg mixture. Mix slightly.

4. Fold in nuts, chocolate chips, and diced bananas.

5. Set your stove to medium heat. Oil a nonstick skillet with cooking spray, and place the pan on the stove. Take ¼ cup of the banana mixture in the bowl and cook.

6. Flip after 10 minutes to cook the other side. Repeat with the rest of the batter.

Nutritional Information

Each pancake contains:

195 cal | 4.4g protein | 23.4g carbs | 1.6g fiber | 10.2g fat | 4.7g sat. fat | 369.5mg sodium

Conclusion

Whether it has to do with health, wealth, or overall happiness, what goes into your mouth plays a significant role in these aspects of your life. It may, in fact, be the most important determinant of success. This is why you should be particular about what and how you eat.

This book has done its job of presenting one of the most favored diets in a comprehensive and balanced way. We defined the DASH diet, broke down what micronutrients and macronutrients are, discussed the importance of family mealtimes, and explained the responsibilities that parents have towards their kids in the kitchen. Finally, we offered various exciting and delicious recipes, which also stay within the DASH guidelines—that is, they're healthy and perfect for your entire family.
If you now feel a sense of kitchen adventure and are looking forward to preparing loving memories with your kids, then DASH Kids Lunch Break was a success!

Thank you for not only purchasing this book, but also spending another currency that is even more valuable than money: your time. Hopefully, you enjoyed reading this book as much as I did writing it.
If you feel this way, then kindly leave a favorable review.

References

- Abramovitz, A. B. & Birch, L. L. (2000). Five-year-old girls' ideas about dieting are predicted by their mothers' dieting. Journal of The American Dietetic Association, 100(10), 1157-1163. https://10.1016/S0002-8223(00)00339-4

- Alhussain, M. H., Macdonald, I. A., & Taylor, M. A. (2016). Irregular meal-pattern effects on energy expenditure, metabolism, and appetite regulation: a randomized controlled trial in healthy normal-weight women. The American journal of clinical nutrition, 104(1), 21–32. https://doi.org/10.3945/ajcn.115.125401

- All the images in this book are sourced from Pixabay

- Bailey, L. (2018). Parents: think twice before you pressure your picky eater. Michigan News. https://news.umich.edu/parents-think-twice-before-you-pressure-your-picky-eater/

- Centers for Disease Control and Prevention. (2019, June 24). Childhood Obesity Facts. Centers for Disease Control and Prevention. https://www.cdc.gov/obesity/data/childhood.html.

- Children's Hospital of Philadelphia. (n.d.). School Aged Child Nutrition. https://www.chop.edu/conditions-diseases/school-aged-child-nutrition#

- Curran, S. (2019). Eating together-eating well: pivoting the picky eater. Rutgers. https://njaes.rutgers.edu/fs1304/

- Fisher, O. J. & Birch, L. L. (1999). Restricting access to palatable foods affects children's behavioral response, food selection, and intake. The American Journal of Clinical Nutrition, 69(6), 1264-1272. https://doi.org/10.1093/ajcn/69.6.1264

- Fryar CD, Hughes JP, Herrick KA, Ahluwalia, N. (2018). Fast food consumption among adults in the United States, 2013–2016. NCHS Data Brief, no 322. Hyattsville, MD: National Center for Health Statistics. https://www.cdc.gov/nchs/data/databriefs/db322-h.pdf

- Government of Canada. (2019, December 12). Healthy eating recommendations. Canada's food guide. https://food-guide.canada.ca/en/healthy-eating-recommendations/cook-more-often/involve-others-in-planning-and-preparing-meals/involving-kids-in-planning-and-preparing-meals/.
- Harvard Health Publishing. (2014, November). Eating fish linked to fewer heart

- attacks. Harvard Health. https://www.health.harvard.edu/heart-health/eating-fish-linked-to-fewer-heart-attacks.

  Harvard Medical School. (2018). Eating five servings of fruits and vegetables can go a long way to protecting against

  heart disease and cancer. https://www.health.harvard.edu/staying-healthy/getting-your-five-a-day

- Maze, J. (2018). Here's who eats fast food, according to the CDC. Restaurant Business. https://www.google.com/amp/s/www.restaurantbusinessonline.com/amp/financing/who-eats-fast-food-according-cdc

- Paoli, A., Tinsley, G., Bianco, A., & Moro, T. (2019). The Influence of Meal Frequency and Timing on Health in Humans: The Role of Fasting. Nutrients, 11(4), 719. https://doi.org/10.3390/nu11040719

- Parker-Pope, T. (2008, September 14). 6 Food Mistakes Parents Make. The New York Times. https://www.nytimes.com/2008/09/15/health/healthspecial2/15eat.html.

- Salamon, M. (2011). Know what's creating young picky eaters? Pressure to eat. Live Science. https://www.google.com/amp/s/www.livescience.com/amp/16222-pressure-eat-creates-picky-eaters.html

- Sandoval, K. (2020, August 14). Kids in the U.S. are eating more fast food, the CDC reports. NBCNews.com. https://www.nbcnews.com/health/kids-health/kids-u-s-are-eating-more-fast-food-cdc-reports-n1236756.

- Schuna, C. (n.d.). Why is lunch so important? Livestrong. https://www.livestrong.com/article/449208-why-is-lunch-so-important/

- Smith, D. K. (2020). 4 reasons your kid needs a healthy school lunch. 100 Days of Real Food. https://www.100daysofrealfood.com/benefits-healthy-school-lunch/

- Wexler, S. (2017). Exercise vs diet: the truth about weight loss. Huffpost. https://www.google.com/amp/s/m.huffpost.com/us/entry/5207271/amp

- World Health Organization. (2019, September 13). Hypertension. Retrieved December 28, 2020, from https://www.who.int/news-room/fact-sheets/detail/hypertension
-

www.ingramcontent.com/pod-product-compliance
Lightning Source LLC
Chambersburg PA
CBHW021426070526
44577CB00001B/86